# CASTLES OF GOD

*Fortified Religious Buildings of the World*

First published 2004

The Boydell Press is an imprint of Boydell & Brewer Ltd
PO Box 9, Woodbridge, Suffolk IP12 3DF, UK
and of Boydell & Brewer Inc.
668 Mt. Hope Avenue, Rochester, NY 14620, USA
website: www.boydellandbrewer.com

ISBN 1 84383 066 3

A CIP catalogue record for this book is available
from the British Library

Library of Congress Cataloging-in-Publication Data

Harrison, Peter, 1941 Apr. 17–
  Castles of God: fortified religious buildings of the world / Peter Harrison.
    p. cm.
Includes bibliographical references and index.
ISBN 1-84383-066-3 (hardback : alk. paper)
1. Fortress-churches. 2. Fortification. 3. Religious institutions. I. Title.

NA4800.H34 2004
736'.09'02–dc22
                            2004000372

This publication is printed on acid-free paper

Printed in the United Kingdom at the
University Press, Cambridge

# CONTENTS

# INTRODUCTION

Religion and fortification have been intertwined since antiquity. Yet the subject has been little studied or understood. Writers on religion, whether from a theological, historical or architectural perspective, make only passing reference; similarly writers on military architecture have tended to ignore religious fortifications and show little recognition of their role and importance. Military and religious architecture have, in the main, been treated as entirely different subjects. It is hard to understand why.

Large numbers of religious buildings with varying degrees of fortification still remain today. They are ubiquitous throughout the Old and New Worlds, the Orient and the Occident, their significance and role in history unrecognised and unrecorded.

Bernard Rudofsky through his book *The Prodigious Builders* first introduced me to the concept of a fortress church. He had set out to document 'non-pedigreed architecture', his book containing 'notes towards a natural history of architecture with special regard to those species that are traditionally neglected or downright ignored'.[1] A few pages were devoted to what he calls 'those least-known manifestations of peasant genius, the Transylvanian village fortresses', where he used as his examples the fortress churches of Harman and Prejmer in Romania, both of them churches surrounded by powerful fortifications.

An opportunity in 1989 to travel through Romania enabled me to visit some of these churches. I was immediately struck by their number, the vast energy and resources expended in their construction and, not least, the impact they made on the landscape. It was an inquisitiveness to know more about these fortress churches, which at that time I thought were unique, that provided the stimulus for further research that has resulted in this book. In writing it I have had, broadly speaking, two main aims: firstly to proselytise, raising awareness and interest, and secondly to encourage further examination and exploration.

So far my findings lead me to believe that the greater majority of the world's religious fortifications are Christian and that it was the dawning of monasticism which resulted in the need. It is thus appropriate to begin this study with the acceptance of Christianity as the official religion of the Roman Empire in 313, as it was not long before monasteries in Palestine and Egypt began to fortify. This led to an architectural process that was to continue for around 1500 years, finally ending in the late eighteenth and early nineteenth centuries when the mendicant friars fortified their missions in what are now the south-western states of America, and Russian colonists in Siberia surrounded their churches with wooden stockades.

Although Christianity is pre-eminent in the number and variety of its fortified religious establishments, adherents of other faiths, in particular Muslims and Buddhists, have felt the need to fortify some of their monasteries, and these will be discussed in this volume.

It is true to say that much research develops and expands due to chance discovery and good fortune, and mine has been no exception. However, it is, I feel, necessary to mention the

---

[1] Rudofsky (1977). This is his subtitle to *The Prodigious Builders*.

problems encountered in the gathering of the material over the last decade and the difficulties faced in the presentation of what appears to be such a diverse and disparate subject, not least in an endeavour to try to excuse those mistakes and errors that are inevitable in a book of this scope.

I am extremely fortunate that I have been able to visit many of the sites mentioned in the text. Fieldwork, however, has its own limitations. Great Britain has a high regard for its architectural heritage emulated until recently by few countries and has the will and finance to preserve its legacy from the past. In many countries the destruction and ruination of countless religious buildings has continued unabated, frequently due to the forces of nature (earthquakes in Armenia, fires in Bhutanese dzongs), or to the dictates of politics.

# The literature

Few authors have concentrated exclusively on religious fortifications and the majority of those who have done so have tended to focus on a narrow regional or parochial viewpoint.[2] The concomitant linguistic problems, that in many instances are insurmountable, have led, even when there are brief English summaries, to an isolation of knowledge.[3] Additionally, the paucity and depth of literature published in English has resulted in a lack of accumulated knowledge so freely available to the ecclesiologist and the castelologist. There are signs that things are changing, and the bibliography shows that over the last few years more authors are turning their attention to aspects of ecclesiastical fortification. Paradoxically, the nineteenth and early-twentieth-century journals of intrepid Victorian and Edwardian travellers have proved unexpected but valuable sources, particularly for the fortified monasteries of the Balkans, Palestine, Egypt and Bhutan, not least because of the splendid engravings and early photographs they contain.

The study of Islamic architecture is still in its infancy, although writers are increasingly addressing the subject. In particular mention should be made of Robert Hillenbrand's book *Islamic Architecture* and that of his wife Carole who writes about the Islamic perspective of the Crusades. I have found both books stimulating and instructive. Of value too is *Architecture of the Islamic World*, edited by George Michell, the gazetteer being especially helpful as an aid to fieldwork.

Similarly, works on the architecture of Buddhist monasteries are few; however, the books by White, Hosla and Aris have proved invaluable.

[2] Sheila Bonde is, as far as I have discovered, the first academic writing in English to treat the subject in a challenging, wide-ranging and erudite way, looking as she does beyond her locality of south-western France. She devotes however almost three-quarters of her book (1994) to the discussion of three fortified churches.

[3] *The History of Armenian Architecture* by Varazdat Harlityunian, for example, is well illustrated with photographs and plans and was an invaluable aid with fieldwork in that country. Frustratingly, there is not a word in any other language than Armenian.

# Presentation

In an endeavour to present the subject of religion and fortification in a meaningful way the needs and responses of three of the great religions of the world have to be identified and understood. The background diversity of the geography, politics, history and time scale all need to be examined, if often briefly, to make sense of the complexity of the subject, a complexity compounded by the variety of the architectural typologies that need to be described.

To try to give an understanding of this relatively unknown and increasingly complex subject the book is divided into three sections. Whilst each of the three religions under consideration is dealt with separately a common simplified basic typology can be followed in each case. Monasteries are found in Christendom, the lands of Islam and the Buddhist territories of the Himalayas, Tibet and China. Similarly some of the various orders, sects and schools developed their monasteries to provide for their specific needs. There are similarities of purpose.

Some understanding of the reasons behind the fusion of fortification with religion is mandatory. Space limitation necessitates brevity, but why religious buildings were fortified remains as important as how they were.

A chronological approach to each section has been adopted to give a historical understanding behind the decision to fortify and the differing approaches to achieve this. Necessary diversions, occasionally into isolated and fascinating backwaters, for example the enigmatic Irish monastic round towers and the eighteenth-century fortifications of much earlier churches of the Islamic Caucasus will, I believe, add to an understanding of regional variations.

As previously stated, the bulk of ecclesiastical fortifications are Christian and the greatest proportion of the book is devoted to them. The large numbers studied lend, at times, to a generic rather than specific approach. There is a disproportionate amount of material available for each religion and although typologically they stand comparison, the sheer numbers and regional variations that exist in Christian countries is not replicated in Islamic and Buddhist regions; there simply was not the necessity.

The approach to Islamic religious fortifications is more focused and specific; numbers are much less and choice limited. Much attention has to be given to the ribat and its Holy Warriors, not least because it was the forerunner of its genre. Consideration of the castles of the Assassins, the Nizari Ismailis, penetrates one of those backwaters previously mentioned.

The section on the Buddhist monasteries in the Himalayas and Tibet has been by far the most difficult to research and write about and epitomises all the problems previously mentioned.

The many hundreds of place names encountered in the course of research have presented particular problems, as sources are not only of disparate age and quality, but also contradictory, and reliable forms are often almost impossible to come by. The names have been checked as far as possible for accuracy and consistency, but imprecise forms are regrettably bound to persist to some extent.

# General architectural features

The scope of this book precludes a detailed classification of the huge numbers of fortified religious buildings. There are, however, a number of generalisations that may be regarded as an early and embryonic attempt to categorise religious fortifications. Two main criteria need to be satisfied: the spiritual role of the building or complex must be at least as great as its secular and military role, and either archival or architectural evidence of fortification must be available or present.

The majority of religious buildings that were fortified by the addition of conventional military architecture of the relevant era can be subdivided into three main groups. Firstly there are religious buildings that themselves were not fortified but were surrounded by a defensive enceinte. Secondly there are those that were built originally without any attempt to fortify being made but were subsequently to receive fortifications with the addition of towers, battlements, loop-holes, fortified residences and other forms of military architecture. The third grouping contains those religious establishments that received a combination of both forms of fortification. In essence, the original ecclesiastical building or complex was first constructed without defence being a prime consideration. As a consequence almost every conceivable form of religious edifice can be found with evidence of fortification; moreover, almost all forms of military architecture were used in their fortification. Churches in particular lent themselves to be fortified in a great variety of ways, sometimes over long periods of time.

There are, however, a number of distinct architectural types that were developed specifically by each of the three religions in response to a perceived need for fortification. The result is a fusion of religious and military architecture. These new forms of architecture were designed and built to serve a specific purpose created by changing political circumstances. These distinct types will be considered in the course of the book.

# The principles of selection

When choosing fortified religious buildings for description and discussion in some detail a variety of criteria were used and a number of difficulties encountered in their selection, not least the sheer numbers to choose from.

Paramount has been the decision to include only buildings where the religious role had at least equal prominence with any other function, especially the military use, and where, architecturally, the ecclesiastical edifice is subservient to the military. Thus the conventual castles of the military orders in the Holy Land, northern Europe and the Iberian peninsula are included. Many would argue that these fortifications are, in reality, castles. Certainly they satisfy the definition of a castle as 'a large building or set of buildings fortified for defence'.[4] What distinguishes them from the thousands of fortresses and castles to be found throughout the world is the role that Christianity and religion played in their design, construction, function and garrisoning. The Crac des Chevaliers is probably one of the most famous castles in the world, recognised by almost every student of military architecture for its mediaeval complexity.

---

[4] *Shorter Oxford English Dictionary.*

What is not usually appreciated is that the inner enceinte contains a monastic core of knights' hall, dormitory, cloister and chapel; here the warrior monk was totally isolated from the outside world and lived a life that could be separated from lay servants and mercenary soldiers. Similarly, in every instance where a castle is redefined as a religious fortification the castle or fortress commander was always a man of high religious standing with religion playing a pivotal role, whether the fortifications were built by Christians, Muslims or Buddhists.

The great majority of the various religious fortifications described in the narrative have been visited, with the exception of the New World and Scandinavia. This was a positive decision to understand the ambient nature of fortification when fused with religious architecture. Many book descriptions do not adequately convey this fusion of the two forms of architecture and the aura and power of ecclesiastical and religious fortifications. Exploration of the church of Saint-Pierrevillers, near Verdun in France, gives a tremendous insight into the way that the devout of this small farming hamlet tried to defend their community in the sixteenth century. Salvation needed to be as secular as it was religious. The hugely imposing dzong at Trongsa, in the middle of Bhutan, with its protective forts is an awesome fortification even today. Yet there is warmth and joy here, where the Buddhist monks welcome people to their service and transform their fortress into something sacred and soul-inspiring with their cymbals, drums, trumpets and chanting of mantras. It is hard to believe that this was not always the case. At the other end of the scale an afternoon of fieldwork and survey in Northumberland at the Vicar's Pele tower at Corbridge showed how this small defence tower in the churchyard was made as comfortable as possible for its occupants.

Where possible the best existing examples are described to demonstrate not only the fusion of ecclesiastical and military architecture, but also how one can harmonise and blend with the other. This is best seen in France where some of the Romanesque churches have late mediaeval military architecture imposed upon them. This is especially true in La Thiérache in the north where the marriage of redbrick defences and white limestone church is architecturally pleasing. There again, the austere and powerful fortress cathedral in Coimbra in Portugal does what it was intended to do, overawe and dominate not only its town but also its congregation.

Similarly where a generic type is instantly recognisable, as exemplified by the Irish round towers and the La Thiérache churches, differing forms have been chosen to demonstrate architectural variation within the genus. The same holds true when regional differences in the fortified churches of France are discussed.

Conversely when the remaining examples of the ribat are compared with recent archaeological discoveries in Monastir in Tunisia a uniformity of design and style is clearly demonstrated.

With the conventual castles of the military orders an attempt has been made to choose examples that show how the castle was adapted to the needs of a new type of garrison and how it developed further. They had to include the ecclesiastical buildings needed for this new type of Christian warrior which resulted in a prototype of a concentric castle reaching its final development in the Holy Land at the Crac des Chevaliers.

The historical context is also very important and a number of monasteries have been chosen for the role they played in national defence and determination at a time when a country was at its lowest ebb. The first dzong built by the Shabdrung at Simtokha in Bhutan, the Mont St Michel in France and the monastery of the Holy Trinity and St Sergius at Zagorsk in Russia all proved very successful when these nations were under sustained attack. Others, especially in Crete and the Balkans, were involved in the wars of liberation against the forces of the Ottoman Empire.

A number of examples are included because they are unique. The Potala Palace of the Dalai Lama is one of the world's greatest buildings and combines monumental fortifications with the most powerful of religious imagery, mirrored perhaps only by the Vatican as the ultimate in ecclesiastical power. Many of the monasteries of Moldavia in Romania were fortified as part of a defensive chain to protect the region against the Turks and the Crimean Tatars. As well as being true fortress monasteries they are unique for the vibrancy and expressionism of the frescoes painted both on the inside and the outside walls of their monastic churches depicting mediaeval propaganda at its finest. Similarly, examples are included where their architecture contains unique features. The arcades introduced by David the Builder into his fortified palaces in Pembrokeshire in south-west Wales are limited to a very few buildings and not found outside the land holdings of the bishopric.

In a number of instances, surprisingly separated by centuries and on two continents, in addition to monastic defences, fortifications were added to those of the monastery for the specific protection of the local population under its physical as well as spiritual care. The finest example in Europe is to be found in Ireland at the Augustinian priory of Kells in Co. Kilkenny where the fortified enceinte of the priory has attached to it a huge outer bailey still surrounded by its curtain wall and tower-houses. In a similar way, but much less sophisticated and built centuries later, the missions in La Bahia in Texas had an attached fortified compound to protect native American converts from the Apaches and Comanches.

Many countries in the Christian West contain large numbers of fortified churches, especially France, Austria and Romania. From these countries exemplar churches have been chosen to show how and why these parish churches were fortified and to indicate the effort put in by the peasant and artisan communities to protect themselves when there was nobody else to do it for them. In addition the various forms of military architecture used, varying between the encircled churches of Transylvania and the fortified round-tower churches of Scandinavia are analysed to illustrate the differing forms of military architecture.

Some countries are covered in more detail than others in comparison to the number of ecclesiastical fortifications they contain: Armenia, Georgia and Ethiopia can be singled out. They warrant a disproportionate consideration because of the remoteness of their ecclesiastical fortifications, their lack of recognition, even in their own countries, and the almost total lack of literature available in English.

# 1
# MIDDLE EASTERN ORIGINS

## Origins

Roman persecution of Christians under the emperor Diocletian in the third century resulted in a way of life and a form of architecture which has not only endured to this day but has barely changed in concept and form. The deserts of Egypt and Palestine had long provided an environment where men and women could lead a life of isolation, seclusion and contemplation. This process of anchoresis (the leading of an eremitic existence, mainly for religious reasons) burgeoned when Diocletian, who, supported by the army, seized control of the empire in 284, sought to bring about reforms. These were not universally welcomed in all the provinces of the empire; Egypt in particular opposed them. Believing Christians to be the subversive element, Diocletian set about persecuting, to the extreme, the faith he believed responsible for this opposition. In Egypt and Palestine what had been a trickle of anchorites into the deserts became a flood.

Christian anchorites started meeting together on Saturdays, Sundays and holy days for spiritual guidance and communal services, returning to their isolated caves, cells and hermitages the rest of the week for solitary contemplation and meditation. Thus developed the laura, the origin of the Christian monastery. A meeting place, a central church, a kitchen and a refectory were needed and came to be grouped together. Even when all fear of persecution had been removed, few of these early monks returned to their previous lives and environments.

This laura system of monastic retreat was taken to Palestine, where it was to remain the favoured form of monasticism. In Egypt, however, there was a significant departure. Pachomius, a retired soldier from Thebes, in an endeavour to establish a pious, enlightened and self-sufficient community, an example to others developed the first monastery where his followers shared a communal life separated from the outside world by a walled compound containing communal buildings. The individual living quarters or cells were now close to each other, the refectory and the church. The necessary kitchen, store-rooms and workshops completed the complex and formed the coenobitical or communal-life monastery.[1]

This form of monasticism flourished and spread to Asia Minor, where, as in Egypt, it predominated. Building arrangements and structural relationships were haphazard, however, and never achieved the uniform and formalised characteristics of later Western European monasticism.

The enlightened emperor Justinian I, by granting to the monasteries the rights to endowments, legacies and gifts, encouraged the spread and development of monastic life, of which the full extent is only now becoming fully understood as a consequence of recent archaeological investigation of newly discovered sites.[2]

[1] Kamil (1996: 27).    [2] Tribe (1996: 6–10).

Monasticism is not the preserve of Chritianity, however, and its development may well have been influenced by pre-Christian groups, especially the Essenes in Palestine, although the connection is not yet clear.[3] For some two hundred years the Essenes had a monastery-like settlement at **Qumran** in Judaea. Famed for the discovery in 1947 of the first of the Dead Sea scrolls in a cave above the settlement, Qumran came into existence around 150 BC as a centre, apparently for the Essenes, an ascetic and messianic Jewish group formed to oppose the Hellenistic influence upon Jewish temple rites. Devoutly religious, the Essenes devoted themselves to a life centred upon prayer, study of the Old Testament and purity of mind and soul. Whilst never gaining a wide following, the community was able to maintain its self-sufficiency and ascetic qualities until the Roman army dispersed the sect in AD 68 during the Jewish revolt against Rome.

Following the discovery of the Dead Sea scrolls R. de Vaux and his team of French archaeologists excavated the area between 1951 and 1956, when the settlement layout was exposed and further scrolls found. It is postulated that not only did the Essenes play an important role in preparing the Jews for the coming of Christ but also significantly influenced the rules affecting later monastic orders, eastern and western.

Perched on a small plateau above the north-west shore of the Dead Sea in the harshly beautiful rolling hills of the Judaean desert, the excavated settlement is trapezoidal in shape, covering an area approximately 100 x 80m. Although dry and arid today water played an important role in the daily life of the community and an aqueduct brought water from a dam constructed in the neighbouring Wadi Qumran. An ingenious system of settling tanks and connecting channels enabled clean water to be distributed throughout the settlement and stored in cisterns and reservoirs. Bathing was an important part of Essene ritual, and two baths at the opposing north-west and south-east ends of the settlement have been identified.

The largest, most substantial and imposing building in the commune is, however, the rectangular, two-storey defence tower measuring 16 x 12m, positioned in the middle of the northern boundary wall, the least defensible part of the site. Still standing to a height of almost 10m, the amount of masonry debris around the tower suggests that originally it arose to a far greater height and would have provided a vantage ground for the surveillance of the surrounding desert and a refuge for the community. It is the first indication that such communities needed a place of safety, in this instance from the surrounding nomadic population. Next to the refectory the archaeologists discovered a pottery workshop and kilns where the seven hundred plates, bowls and cups found in the refectory annex were made. Strangely the kitchen is located some distance away from the refectory. Located next to the council chamber, between the tower and the refectory, was the scriptorium, still containing inkpots when uncovered, and almost certainly where the Dead Sea scrolls were written. The settlement was enclosed on the south and west by the cliff edge of the plateau, and by walls to the north and east. The surrounding area is riddled with caves, and given the absence of houses or cells in the compound it is believed that many of the community utilised them to live in. Essentially a farming community, the presence of cattle and sheep pens suggests self-sufficiency. Used as a garrisoned fortress by the Romans during the siege of Masada until its fall in 74 and

[3] Badawy (1978: 35).

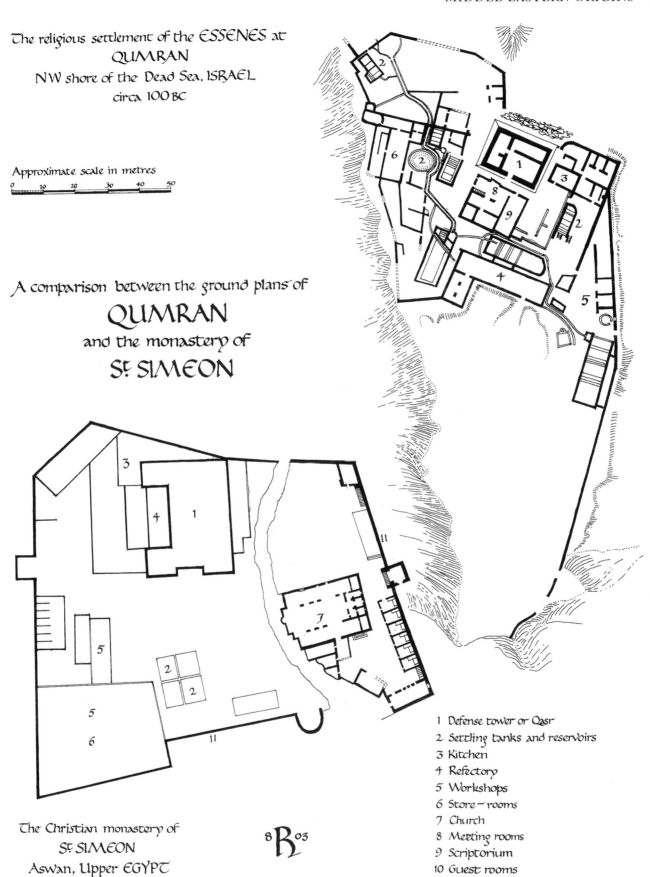

The religious settlement of the ESSENES at
QUMRAN
NW shore of the Dead Sea, ISRAEL
circa 100 BC

Approximate scale in metres

0    10    20    30    40    50

A comparison between the ground plans of
QUMRAN
and the monastery of
S.ᵗ SIMEON

The Christian monastery of
S.ᵗ SIMEON
Aswan, Upper EGYPT
circa 12ᵗʰ

8 B 03

1 Defense tower or Qasr
2 Settling tanks and reservoirs
3 Kitchen
4 Refectory
5 Workshops
6 Store ~ rooms
7 Church
8 Meeting rooms
9 Scriptorium
10 Guest rooms
11 Fortified enceinte

again during the Bar Kochba revolt between 132 and 135, the site was abandoned shortly afterwards.

Qumran may well have influenced the coenobitical architecture that was to develop some two to three hundred years later. Hirschfeld describes the settlement of monks in fortresses that had been vacated by the Romans in Syria and Palestine and mentions that Anthony, one of the early monastic founders in Egypt, lived for a number of years in one such fortress. He postulates that the remote position, lack of ownership and an established water source were attractive to the early monks.[4] By these criteria Qumran would be attractive to early anchorites. In a similar way, and at the same time, the Egyptian anchorites were colonising abandoned Pharaonic and Roman buildings.

## The fortified Coptic monasteries

The early Eastern coenobitical monasteries in particular varied in size from comparatively small units to huge complexes, but the basic plan is that of Qumran with the addition of churches, chapels and cells. Most were girdled with a wall but this was more for statement than defence; a symbol of rejection by the communal monastic population of the secular world outside, whose threat was perceived as moral and psychological rather than physical. And yet physical threat always existed, especially where, despite individual vows of poverty, the collective monastery became increasingly wealthy from legacies, donations, produce from its workshops and the increasingly lucrative pilgrimage trade. The more pragmatic communities recognised that a physical shelter and refuge was needed for their safety and that geographical isolation and the protection afforded by relics could not always be relied upon. As a consequence substantial towers, primarily for defence, are to be found in many of the early monasteries which still have physical remains.

That such towers were needed in Egypt is recorded in the Ethiopian *Synaxarium*, the book of saints, which tells of barbarians slaying the monks and plundering the monasteries of Sketis in Lower Egypt. It records that Abba John fled to the monastery of Abba Anthony in the desert of Kuelzem by the Red Sea. This perhaps implies that the former monasteries were indefensible but the later was not.

The whole of the Nile valley from Aswan to the delta contains many ruins of monasteries fortified in this way. The qasr, the final retreat and refuge (which predates the Norman keep by centuries), is either incorporated into or surrounded by a high and robust wall with a wall walk but rarely reinforced by corner or interval towers. The solitary narrow entrance is occasionally defended by a projecting box machicolation and barred by wooden beams or a wheel stone. These unsophisticated defences could never resist any determined or sustained assault by large numbers but they were efficient in protecting the monks against brigands and desert nomads.

In the desert of Upper Egypt, just inland from the west bank of the Nile, opposite the town of Aswan, lies the monastery of **St Simeon**. Although founded in the seventh century, the present ruins date from the tenth century. Despite being built on two levels the ground plan bears a similarity to that of Qumran in that it is trapezoidal in shape and of approximately

---

[4] Hirschfeld (1992: 47–9).

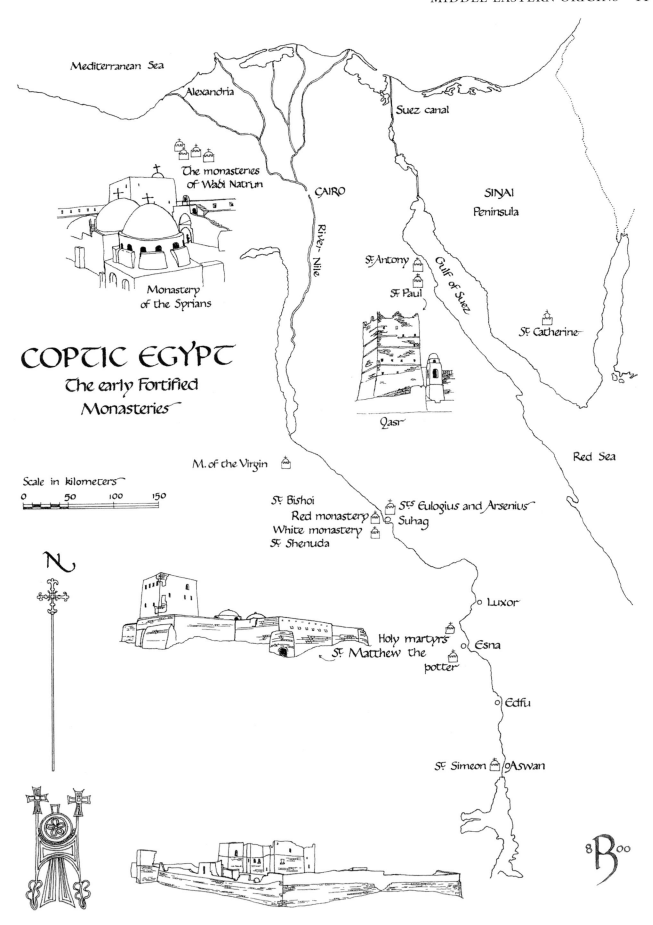

Mediterranean Sea

Alexandria

Suez canal

CAIRO

SINAI
Peninsula

The monasteries
of Wadi Natrun

Monastery
of the Sprians

St Antony

St Paul

Gulf of Suez

St Catherine

# COPTIC EGYPT
The early Fortified
Monasteries

Qasr

Red Sea

M. of the Virgin

Scale in kilometers

0    50    100    150

St Bishoi
Red monastery
White monastery
St Shenuda

Sts Eulogius and Arsenius
Suhag

N

Luxor

Holy martyrs
St Matthew the
potter

Esna

Edfu

St Simeon    Aswan

8 Roo

the same size. In addition to a Christian church and chapels the enclosed courtyard contains the refectory, kitchen, store-rooms and workshops, and water channels lead to settlement tanks and cisterns. It is still surrounded by its defensive wall, over 6m high in places, and a huge defensive tower forms part of the northern defences. The solitary entrance is through a small tower in the eastern wall and the whole monastery has foundations and lower courses of stone with mud-brick superstructures.[5]

### The monasteries of the Wadi al-Natrun

The monasteries of Sketis were founded by Makarius, a disciple of Anthony, around 330, and subsequently sacked by Berbers in 404, 434 and 444 (which may have given rise to the building of the first Christian qasrs). The region is now known as the Wadi al-Natrun, named after the various salts deposited in the valley and its lakes. It lies 75km north-west of Cairo and is a natural depression in the desert running diagonally south-east to north-west for approximately 50km, although never more than 8km wide. Although once heavily populated with monks in many monasteries and their dependencies, it has never recovered from the great plagues that struck Egypt in the fourteenth century. Today only four monasteries remain that are not utterly ruined, all located near to each other on the lower slope on the south-west side of the valley. The monastery of **St Makarius** lies in the east, followed by **St Bishoi's**, then the monastery of the **Syrians**, and lastly that of the **Romans** in the north-west of the valley. Each is fortified, shows a similarity of design and contains a qasr. As a result of further sackings both before and after the Arab invasion of the seventh century no remains earlier than the ninth century can be identified today. Following the destruction by the desert tribes in 817 the monasteries of the Wadi al-Natrun began to fortify themselves in earnest.

The four monasteries of the Wadi al-Natrun demonstrate the development of the qasr. Although dating is difficult, it is likely that the tower at the monastery of the Romans is the earliest and simplest and that of St Makarius the most sophisticated. All are strongly built either of stone or mud brick on a stone base and are the most substantial of all the monastic buildings. Usually three storeys high and either square or rectangular, access is via a narrow wooden drawbridge that when raised fits into the recessed masonry surrounding the first-storey doorway. Each storey with the possible exception of the uppermost contains a central corridor with barrel-vaulted chambers on either side, acting as store-rooms, dormitory and refectory. There was usually provision for a strongroom to safeguard the treasures of the monastery, relics and sacred objects; the basement well provided a water source. Every qasr had at least one chapel or church, usually on the uppermost floor, dedicated either to the archangel Michael, to one of the warrior saints, or to the Virgin Mary. The ground plan averages 20 x 15m and the walls are up to 2m thick; where present, windows are high, narrow and splayed. Between 15 and 20m high, the qasr dominates the monastery, the gateway and the enceinte. Last century archaeologists working in the valley uncovered the foundations of

---

[5] Although slighted on the orders of Saladin in 1173 in order to deny its use to Nubian Christians, who were intent on raiding southern Egypt, it still retains many of its buildings to their full height. The monastery gives great insight into the typology of early Egyptian monasteries, although many of the buildings of today are from the high Middle Ages.

*The Coptic Monasteries of the*
# WADI al-NATRUN
## Lower EGYPT

1 *Dair Abu Maqar* 1

*St Makarius*

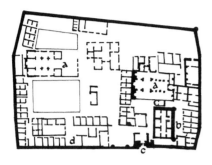

2 *Dair al-Baramus* 2

*Monastery of the Romans*

3 *Dair al Syrian – monastery of the Sprians*

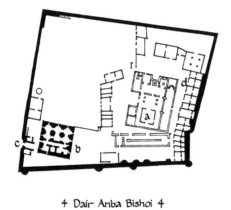

4 *Dair Anba Bishoi* 4

*St Bishoi*

a  Church
b  Qasr
c  Gateway
d  Cells

Alexandria

Desert of Scetis

2
  3 4 1
Natrun valley

Cairo

Section and floor plans
of the QASR of the
Dair al Syrian

ground

much smaller walled enclosures, each with an attached tower. They are believed to be the remains of mashubeh, small fortified dwellings for monks living separately from their mother monastery.[6]

Surrounded by farmland containing orchards, pastures and vineyards the monasteries became very wealthy, especially when the remains of the founding saints were identified. The patriarch of the Coptic Church was frequently chosen from one of the monastic abbots and the monasteries were kept in a good state of repair, especially during periods of persecution when they were used by the Church hierarchy as refuges.

At the monastery of **St Makarius**, always the most important foundation in the Wadi al-Natrun and probably in Egypt, Patriarch Shenudeh surrounded the principal church and the other monastery buildings with high towers and strong walls towards the end of the ninth century. The fortifications that remain today are almost certainly from this period. Like so many Egyptian fortified monasteries, it is trapezoidal in shape and originally measured 125 x 120m. Previously the largest of all the monasteries it now covers less than half the area it did when in its prime before the depopulation of the fourteenth century. Patriarch Shenudeh surrounded the monastery with walls high enough to deter the most determined of attackers and provide shelter for refugees. Inside was the monastic church, refectory, kitchen, workshops, a corn mill, oil press, a water supply and cells for the monks, together with a large qasr. Although the range of buildings in all the monasteries is very similar there is no formal arrangement and each monastery has its own internal layout. The refectory was not often used, except on special occasions, and dormitories were never built; the monks ate and slept in their own cells.[7] The enceinte was formed of random rubble and mud brick set in a mud mortar; usually 10 to 12m high and up to 2m thick, both inner and outer surfaces were coated with a lime plaster that hardened to provide a protective coating. The wall walk was provided with a shoulder-high parapet. A feature common to all four monasteries is the siting of the solitary entrance gate near to the defensive tower. The gatehouse contains a barrel-vaulted passage, two guard-rooms and a staircase to the chamber above the passage that leads to a trap door in the apex of the external arched recess of the doorway. Containing a windlass, this trap door could be used to hoist up visitors or supplies when the door was barred.[8]

## The monasteries of Palestine

Two differing forms of the laura monastery, which predominated in Palestine and the Judaean desert, have been identified. Perhaps the most impressive are those which cling to the sides of

---

[6] Lythgoe (1975: 51). The ruins of twenty-seven such mashubeh have been identified within the environs of the monastery of St Makarius. Believed to have been abandoned in the fourteenth century, they were ruinous by the fifteenth.

[7] Lythgoe (1975: 3–16). Although the qasr is now incorporated in the east wall of the monastery, it was free-standing originally.

[8] Lythgoe also suggests that this mechanism could also be used to lift and lower either a portcullis or other form of defensive apparatus for the door. This arrangement is seen in some of the smaller fortifications of the military orders in the Baltic States.

cliffs, some of which appear almost sheer, in stark contrast to those lauras built on flat ground, found mainly in the Jericho valley; the cliff lauras are the most numerous. In contrast, most Palestinian coenobia are found on flat ground, but to complicate matters further one of the best cliff-side monasteries is the monastery of St George (the present-day monastery of **Choziba** in Wadi Qilt, near Jericho), founded in the fifth or sixth century; originally a laura, it was converted into a coenobium. Most of the present building is of nineteenth-century construction but it retains substantial remains from earlier periods and gives a good idea of the defensibility of these monasteries.[9] Even today access is difficult and somewhat perilous.

Although a number of Palestinian monasteries have been reoccupied and partially rebuilt to accommodate those wishing to live a contemplative life the vast majority have been destroyed and are ruinous. Hirschfeld has, however, excavated a number of monasteries in the Judaean desert. From his findings and observations it seems very likely that many Palestinian monasteries had an attached tower of a military nature, either built at their highest point or overlooking the gatehouse. Although, in comparison to the later qasrs of Egypt, they are comparatively slight, often little more than 5m square, they were probably of three storeys and used for a variety of purposes. Often used as dwellings by the monks they also served to demarcate the boundaries and holdings of the monastic community. Their main function, however, was to act as a place of refuge for the unarmed monks, forbidden to defend themselves or their monasteries and as a consequence totally reliant on passive protection.[10]

Justinian set in motion a huge building programme when he became emperor, seeking to defend the borders of his empire, particularly in the vulnerable east where the Sassanian Persians were ever ready to take advantage of weakness.[11] We are fortunate that Procopius, the court historian of Justinian, recorded the nature and extent of this mammoth project in his work *De Aedificiis*. It is clear that as well as military and secular works ecclesiastical architecture received his attention, and the evidence is that church building was revolutionised. A domed, brick-vaulted and centrally planned church, a form that was to spread throughout Eastern Christendom, replaced the basilica.[12] He sought to control the Eastern Church, both in Constantinople and the provinces, by combining barracks, church and travellers' lodgings inside a well-fortified enceinte; further control was exercised by insisting on firm adherence to monastic rules and by regularising the interior layout. This is reflected in Krautheimer's observation that although the early monasteries of Egypt and Syria had been surrounded by a

---

[9] It was abandoned after the Persian invasion of 614 and not rebuilt until 1179 when the Crusaders added a defensive tower to guard it and the road from Jerusalem to Jericho.

[10] Hirschfeld (1992: 171–5).

[11] Hirschfeld (1992: 171) says that there is no evidence to support the claim that fortress or fortified monasteries defended the borders of Byzantium against nomadic raiders. One of the few monastery fortresses in the heartland of Byzantium from this period still identifiable today can be found at Daphni, south of Athens. The remains of the fortified perimeter wall demonstrate the power of Justinian's work; interestingly, they now enclose a church from the eleventh century fortified by the Franks at a later date. Krautheimer suggests that these fortress monasteries became the norm even in peaceful areas.

[12] The basilica plan remained in place in the West beyond the mediaeval period.

wall, it was not until the sixth century that they became fortified, an innovation that must be credited to Justinian.[13]

One monastery that has survived, against all the odds, is the monastery of **St Sabas** in the heart of the Judaean mountains 20km from Bethlehem. Now occupied by Greek Orthodox monks, it claims the distinction of being the only continuously occupied monastery in Palestine. Founded in 492 by St Sabas, it was attacked and sacked by the Persians in 614. It was to achieve prominence when John Damascene, a Christian who had achieved high office as the representative of the Christian subjects of the Umayyad caliph in Damascus, renounced his secular life and entered the monastery in 716 to write the *Source of Knowledge*. Now the greatest of all the Judaean monasteries, it overlooks the River Kidron and climbs up the wadi side. Surrounded by a massive triangular buttressed defensive wall, a multi-storey watchtower was built at the highest point of the monastery at the apex of the triangular walls. These defences dominate totally the monastic compound and are further strengthened by the nearby, but isolated, tower of St Simeon, believed to date from the seventeenth century. Like all the monasteries in Palestine many of its buildings have been rebuilt over the centuries and the defensive walls have not been dated with any accuracy.

The monastery of **St Catherine** in the southern desert of Sinai still retains much of its defences from the sixth century against Arab nomads. The first church, that of the Virgin, was built over the reputed site of the Burning Bush on the orders of Helena, mother of Constantine, in 337. Despite its isolation and vulnerability it became a popular pilgrimage site and its importance was recognised by Justinian I who gave orders for the building of a replacement church for the Virgin followed shortly afterwards by the construction of the basilica of the Transfiguration in 537. Surrounding the monastery with strong walls he provided a garrison of two hundred soldiers drawn from Egypt, Greece and the Balkans, to serve and protect the monastic community and its pilgrim visitors.

Built on the side of a wadi of Mount Sinai, the Mount of Moses, it is an extraordinary sight, its high stone walls harmonising with the craggy mountainside. Only glimpses of the belfry and tiled roof give any hint of the monastic complex built inside. Originally named after the mother of Jesus it was renamed after St Catherine who had been martyred in Alexandria in the fourth century.

The ground plan is, once again, an irregular quadrilateral measuring 85 x 75m and the present walls are between 12 and 15m tall. Built out of massive granite blocks in regular courses, much of the wall, especially in the south-west, remains from the time of Justinian. Repairs after earthquake damage in the early part of the fourteenth century can clearly be seen by the change in the masonry style used. Reinforced by corner and interval towers, both round and rectangular, entry until comparatively recently was by a basket hoisted up to a gallery high in the northern wall. Entry today is via a small postern gate in the west wall of the monastery. Inside is a labyrinth of passages, stairs and buildings, both secular and religious, many of which, although of a later date, occupy the position against the walls of the original conventual and

[13] Krautheimer (1986: 260). The addition of the defensive wall coincided with a regularising of the interior, centred on the church. He also states that 'fortress and monastery were joined in a symbiosis strange only to us'.

# The Monastery of St. Catherine→
## Sinai EGYPT

1 Underground cistern
2 Original entrance
3 St Stephen's well
4 Moses' well
5 Mosque
6 Minaret
7 Church of St Catherine
8 6th century chapel
9 Chapel of the burning bush
10 Tower containing chapel of St George
11 Rere-dorter

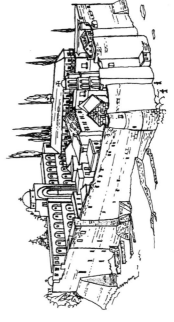

The monastery as it appears today

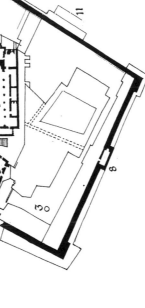

Scale in metres
0 5 10 20 30 40 50

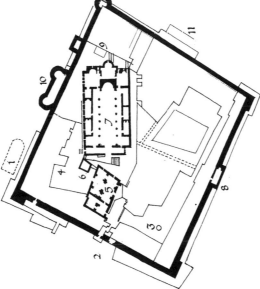

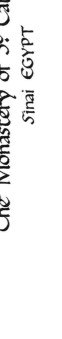

From a medieval painting in the monastery

After a nineteenth century engraving

barrack buildings. Of particular note is the presence within the complex of a mosque. This was converted in 1106 from a hospice both to serve the Islamic servants of the monks and to appease the Muslim rulers in return for their toleration of this important Christian site in the Islamic Empire. The monastery now belongs to the Greek Orthodox Church, and the monks look after a library second only to the Vatican for the number of illuminated manuscripts it contains. It is one of the oldest and most famous of all Christian monasteries and served three functions, monastery, pilgrimage site and desert outpost designed to protect this part of Palestine from the increasingly powerful and bellicose Arabian tribesmen. It is the oldest fortress monastery in existence.

# The fortified pilgrimage sites and the tower churches of Syria

Monasteries had been introduced into Syria from Egypt and followed the basic coenobitical form. Syria had become a prosperous and peaceful province due to the foresight of Justinian; only the borderlands with Persia required much in the way of fortification. More of a problem was the internecine theological conflict which had developed over the monophysite controversy; monophysitism had taken a firm hold in the Near East after its spread from Egypt in the fifth century, posing a substantial threat to the central government-controlled Church. Central government and the Orthodox Church in Constantinople endeavoured to regain full control of the dissident church by lavishing much effort and money in developing shrines to martyrs. Two of the most popular pilgrimage sites that were developed were the cruciform church and monastery of the ascetic St Simeon, near Antioch, and Sergiopolis (Resafeh), on Syria's eastern border, the seat of the cult of St Sergius. Both were fortified, but to different degrees, and became part of the frontier defences of Byzantium along with some of Justinian's fortress monasteries.

Early in the fifth century St Simeon Stylites attracted considerable attention amongst Christians throughout the empire, as much out of curiosity as piety. The emperor Zeno, after Simeon's death, found it politically expedient to pour State resources into the development of this extraordinary pilgrimage site. He built a cruciform church with a central octagonal and domed chamber to surround the stump of the column on top of which St Simeon had spent the last thirty years of his life meditating, musing and entertaining his devotees. Initially fortified in response to threats from the Persians and subsequently the Arabs (it was captured by them in 641) it was refortified when it once again returned to Byzantine rule in the ninth century. Even today in its ruined state it is a very imposing site, situated as it is on the slopes of the Jebel Sema'an, west of Aleppo. The remains of the fortifications are restricted to the lower courses of the enclosure wall and the foundations of a number of towers.

Much more impressive and on a far bigger scale is the fortified pilgrimage town of **Sergiopolis** near the Euphrates in north-east Syria. Originally a Roman frontier fortress built by Diocletian, it became the scene of the martyrdom of Sergius, a Christian Roman soldier who was tortured to death when he refused to sacrifice to Jupiter, Diocletian's preferred religion. His exceptionally brutal murder attracted widespread publicity and increasingly drew pilgrims. Such were the numbers who wished to visit this isolated fort, now containing the martyrium of Sergius, that it had to expand to accommodate the logistical requirements of the pilgrims.

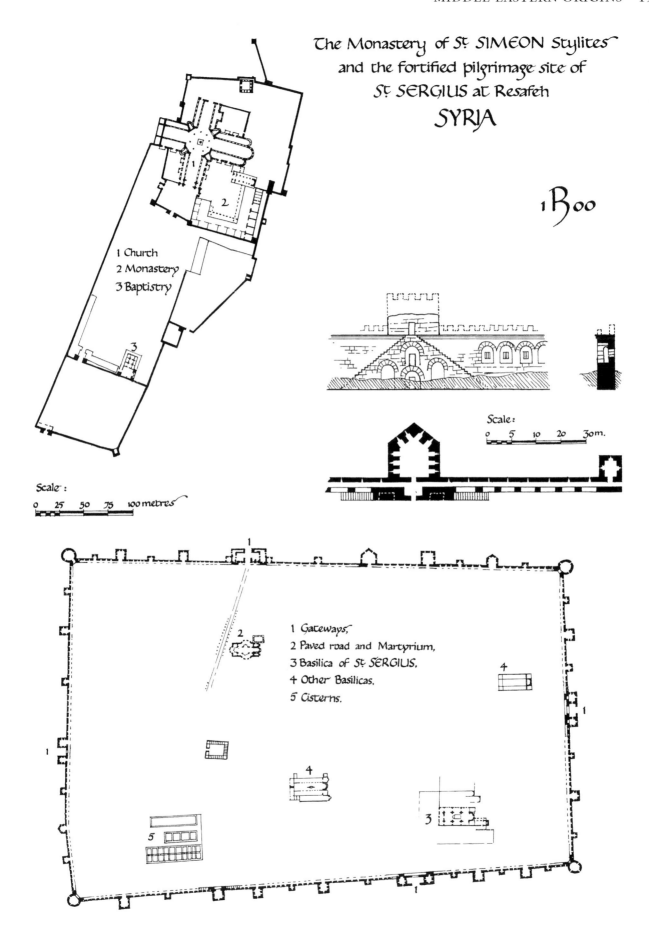

The Monastery of St SIMEON Stylites
and the fortified pilgrimage site of
St SERGIUS at Resafeh
SYRIA

1 Church
2 Monastery
3 Baptistry

Scale :
0    25    50    75    100 metres

Scale :
0   5   10   20   30m.

1 Gateways.
2 Paved road and Martyrium.
3 Basilica of St SERGIUS.
4 Other Basilicas.
5 Cisterns.

The presence of early fortified enclosures is confirmed by the excavations early last century carried out at the monastery of St Jeremiah (Saqqara), destroyed by the Arabs in 960, where the internal arrangements have been found to be very similar to those at St Simeon's.

By the beginning of the seventh century monasticism in the Holy Land and Syria was at its zenith. Pilgrims and aspiring novices travelled from as far afield as Western Europe as well as from all parts of the Byzantine Empire and Transcaucasia to visit the holy sites. The Persian incursion of 614 saw monastery after monastery pillaged and destroyed, and whilst there was some recovery initially the Islamic conquest of 638 in effect saw the demise of monasticism. Although there was little in the way of Arab persecution monasteries were abandoned as recruits and donations dried up, particularly as travel became perilous and pilgrims went elsewhere.

However, one pilgrimage site has survived almost intact for over two thousand years due to the reverence in which it was held by the three religions of the Book. The **cave of Machpelah** in Hebron is believed to be the burial place of the Prophet Abraham, his son Isaac and grandson Jacob, together with their wives, and over the centuries has become a pilgrimage site revered by Jew, Christian and Muslim alike. First fortified by Herod the Great (374 BC) the finely built walls fortify a quadrilateral enclosure measuring 65 x 35m. The great builder Justinian erected a church over the burial site that became the Haram el-Khalil or 'the shrine of the friend' following the Arab conquest, so called because Muslims regard Abraham as the friend of God. Recaptured by the Crusaders, the mosque was converted back to a church only to revert to a mosque once again, which it has remained to this day, when it fell to Baybars in 1267. The Arabs also added two minarets and the present battlements. The original Herodian fortifications remain and the size of the ashlar blocks are cyclopean, especially at the corners of the walls, where the largest measures 7.5 x 1.4m, contributing immensely to the strength of the fortifications. The otherwise plain external faces of the walls are broken by the inclusion of pilasters on all four sides. The only Crusader alterations were the addition of fortifications to defend the Herodian entrance. Like St Saba it is a rare example of ecclesiastical fortification still existing in Judaea. Both, however, give good insight into the efforts made by the early ecclesiastical bodies to defend their establishments.

# 2
# IRELAND

## Introduction

The invasion and the attempted occupation of Ireland in the latter half of the twelfth century by the Anglo-Normans conveniently divides the study of Irish ecclesiastical fortifications into two. Firstly, those built by the Gaelic Irish, in almost total isolation from the rest of the world, and secondly those that were constructed by the Anglo-Normans and their successors. The former produced structures unique to Ireland, the latter, adapting European influences, produced a typology whose function was not seen outside the island.

Prior to the arrival of the Vikings in the ninth century there were few Irish settlements of any size and the population followed a pastoral existence within a clan system. Feuds and cattle-raiding became endemic and the small rural communities responded by protecting themselves within ring-forts found from antiquity throughout Ireland, many thousands of them remaining today. Built mainly of earth and known as a rath, there was a departure in the west and amidst the Atlantic islands where the availability of easily split limestone resulted in the dry-stone ring-fort or cashel. It was into this environment that monasticism arrived, probably from Syria by way of Egypt. By the seventh century a great number of monasteries had been founded and were widespread throughout the island.

## The early Gaelic monasteries

Although archaeological remains from this period are scanty, the western Atlantic coastal region and its islands contain enough stone-built monastic buildings to give a good insight into the nature of these ensembles, which show many similar features. Although there is no formal or set plan, each monastery contains at least one church, an oratory, stone slabs incised with crosses and one or more clochans, the circular beehive-shaped huts for the accommodation of the monks. There was usually a circumvallation to isolate the monastery from the outside world. In most of Ireland wood was used for these buildings and the precinct wall was little more than an earthen bank. In the west stone was used instead; of the surviving examples the finest is to be found on the island of **Inishmurray**, located 6.5km off the Atlantic coast in Co. Sligo. Here the monastic grounds of St Molaise are enclosed by a wall that today is still over 4m high and 2–3m thick. Carefully built of split but undressed limestone this vast dry-stone wall is roughly oval in shape, measuring 45 x 60m. It is very much a cashel, although there are five entrances rather than the usual solitary entry passage. Its interior contains a number of corbelled beehive huts, at least two churches and incised stone slabs, all in a remarkable state of preservation and separated from each other by four walls of varying length and height. It is not known whether the massive encircling wall is contemporary with the early buildings of the monastery and built by the monks or whether they occupied a cashel from an earlier period for

# 3
# THE CRUSADES

## Introduction

The creation during the Crusades of the religious military orders with their communities of armed monks led to a new form of Western military architecture. The desire to live a celibate, religious and reclusive life had to be tempered with the demands of a military role. The orders needed castles, but the castle did not provide the monastic environment that the orders required. The resultant need for a building with two-fold function produced the 'domus conventualis' or conventual castle. Built throughout the Holy Land, the Iberian peninsula, the Baltic and Prussia the architectural form was influenced by military need, the resources available and the support given by Church and State.

For over three hundred years, the conventual castle adapted to changing situations but always maintained its monastic role as long as it was in the ownership of an order. Externally frequently indistinguishable from the secular fortifications of the period, it was the internal arrangements that differed markedly; the monastic plan was always adhered to as far as military considerations allowed.

Wherever the orders went the Church hierarchy was never far behind. When answerable only to the pope, the powers of the orders needed checking and the archbishops and bishops assigned to this task needed their own seats of power, leading, particularly in the Baltic, to the capitular castle or fortified residence of the bishop and his canons.

An offshoot of the Crusades in France and the Iberian peninsula was the fortification of huge cathedrals by their bishops, either as part of a defensive system or as an expression of power.

Finally, in the wake of the Crusades came the re-establishment of the pilgrimage. Often located in vulnerable regions, especially in the Holy Land, the pilgrimage sites needed physical as well as spiritual protection, usually provided by the monastic order entrusted with their safekeeping. Fortification was one of the ways in which this was achieved.

Each of the chosen Crusader regions and periods needs to be examined in turn as, although the basic need for ecclesiastical fortifications was similar, there were considerable variations in the reason, development, manner and style of their construction.

## The Holy Land

For centuries pilgrimage to the Holy Land had been very popular amongst Christians and, on the whole, the Islamic rulers were tolerant, not only of these Western pilgrims, but also of the minority indigenous Christian population. From time to time, however, there were rulers who attempted to interfere with Christian access to the pilgrimage sites. One such was the Fatimid caliph al-Hakim, who destroyed many churches, including the church of the Holy Sepulchre in 1009. Building over the rock of Calvary and the tomb of Jesus caused much shock and distress in Europe, and anger simmered, especially as more and more sacred monuments were destroyed. During Roman and Byzantine times many of the important Holy Places had churches built over them; many now became desecrated.

Coincidentally, the Byzantine emperor, increasingly fearful of the Seljuk Turks after the Byzantine defeat at the Battle of Manzikert in 1071, and without the resources necessary to protect his empire, appealed in March 1095 to Pope Urban II for help.[1] The timing could not have been more fortuitous for Urban.

In the Iberian peninsula Christians had fought Muslims for centuries. The capture of Toledo in Spain in 1085 by King Alphonso VI of León was to prove a turning point in the Christian Reconquest.[2] The opportunity to mobilise Europe against Islam in the Holy Land and the Iberian peninsula was one that Urban quickly seized; he made his 'call to arms' by proclaiming the First Crusade on the 27 November 1095. Such was the enthusiasm of the Christian West to make war on Islam that the first army left for Palestine in early 1096. Reverses and hardship were such that, by the time Jerusalem was captured on 15 July 1099, the granting of mercy was not a consideration for the Crusaders: the Muslim and Jewish populations were brutally massacred.

## *The origins of the military orders of the Templars and the Hospitallers and the development of the conventual castle*

After the capture of Jerusalem, many members of the conquering army went home, leaving the remnant occupying a small area of the Middle East, surrounded on all sides by a hostile and wounded Islamic world. Supplies had to be obtained locally or imported by sea, so helping to re-establish the pilgrim trade. Despite being an occupying force, Christian manpower to defend their acquired lands was woefully short; pilgrimage to Jerusalem remained perilous.

The establishment of Christian states in Palestine and Syria after the First Crusade had not made the roads safe, and the need to protect pilgrims, arriving in ever increasing numbers, led to the formation of the first of the military orders in 1118 by Hugh de Payens. His order of knights combined a protective role towards pilgrims with a strict and celibate religious life. The appropriation of the third-most sacred site of Islam, the Dome of the Rock (Templum Domini, the Temple of the Lord) and the neighbouring Aqsa mosque for the headquarters of the order led it to become known as the Order of the Knights of the Temple, or simply the Templars. The rules of the Cistercians were adopted and the order given papal approval in 1128.

A charitable brotherhood had already existed in Jerusalem before the First Crusade; based at the hospital of St John the Almoner, it served to provide shelter and succour to pilgrims, especially those who became sick. It soon became an independent military order, that of the Knights of St John of Jerusalem, more commonly known as the Hospitallers.

Both orders rapidly acquired both wealth and recruits. The knights became elite, disciplined, highly skilled and permanent brotherhoods of warrior monks. By the middle of the

---

[1] Haldon (2001: 110) points out that it was not so much the military defeat that made Byzantium vulnerable, but rather its civil war that followed the battle.

[2] Riley-Smith (1990: 32).

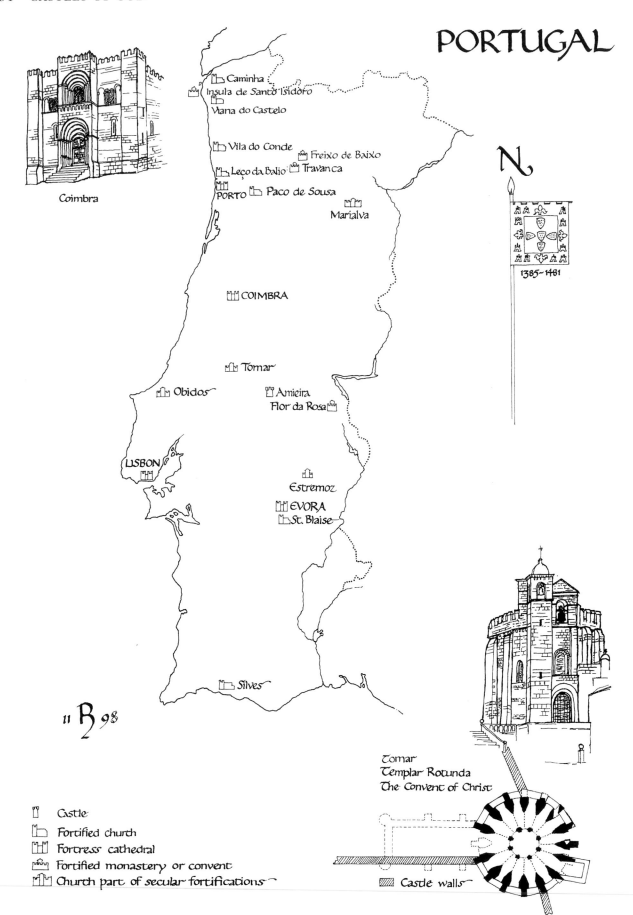

# PORTUGAL

Coimbra

Caminha
Insula de Santo Isidoro
Viana do Castelo

Vila do Conde          Freixo de Baixo
Leço da Balio    Travanca
PORTO    Paço de Sousa
Marialva

1385~1481

COIMBRA

Tomar

Obidos          Amieira
Flor da Rosa

LISBON

Estremoz

EVORA
St. Blaise

11 B 98

Silves

Tomar
Templar Rotunda
The Convent of Christ

Castle
Fortified church
Fortress cathedral
Fortified monastery or convent
Church part of secular fortifications

Castle walls

The towers, façade, nave and, where present, the transepts are surrounded by a crenellated parapet with pointed merlons typical of Moorish military architecture. Above the side aisles runs a gallery serving as a chemin de ronde for the defence of the cathedral church. The nave roofs are barrel-vaulted and support the fighting platform; access to both gallery and roof is reached by two staircases at Coimbra: one in the south-west tower of the façade: the other near the northern joining of the nave and crossing. Both cathedrals have attached cloisters; that at Lisbon is enclosed, in part, with a battlemented wall still remaining and indicating that the cathedral fortifications included the cloister.

Coimbra was completed in 1180, but building work at Lisbon continued into the fourteenth century, following the earthquake of 1340. Whilst expressing the power of archbishop and bishops they played important roles in the defensive system of the kingdom, acting as the citadel of the town where none existed.

## The crusades against the Cathars and the great cathedrals

The dualist beliefs of the heretical Cathars, or Albigensians, who believed that there were two gods, one good, the other totally evil, rose to prominence in south-west France, especially Languedoc, in the twelfth century. By the commencement of the thirteenth century so great was the following amongst the populace, tacitly supported by some noble families and even supposedly orthodox churchmen, that the pope needed to act to counter this threat to the Church of Rome. Catholic supremacy and religious control over a vast tract of land stretching south of a line from Béziers in the east to Bordeaux in the west needed to be re-established.

So great was the perceived threat that when Pope Innocent III called for a crusade in 1208, he exhorted orthodox Christians to 'attack the followers of heresy more fearlessly even than the Saracens, since they are more evil'.[33] Led by Simon de Montefort, the crusading army sacked Béziers, killing Christian and Cathar alike, destroying Cathar churches and strongholds before entering the domains of Count Raymond of Toulouse. The crusade ebbed and flowed over the next two decades until, in 1226, King Louis VIII of France saw his opportunity and invaded the county of Toulouse forcing Raymond to sue for peace, thus ensuring his overlordship of Languedoc. He was quick to encourage orthodox Christian settlers to his new domains, dispossessing the nobility with Cathar sympathies and supporting Cathar persecution by the Inquisition. Whilst these measures contributed to the demise of Catharism in the fourteenth century, the initial response to these actions resulted in a hostile environment, one in which the Church of Rome had to re-establish its authority, both secular and spiritual, in the Cathar heartland. This was achieved in the Languedoc by the building of the great fortress cathedrals of Albi, Narbonne, Lombez, Lodève and Elne, together with the fortified residences of the bishops at Albi and Narbonne.

The red brick town of Albi 'la Rouge', built on the eastern bank of the River Tarn in central Languedoc, is still dwarfed by the great **cathedral of St Cecilia**; a lasting monument to Bernard of Castenet, the second cleric appointed by the pope to the see of Albi. Despite the attention of nineteenth-century restorers it remains today the most complete of these fortress cathedrals.

[33] Barber (2000: 107).

from a very narrow doorway at the southern junction of nave and tower. Defence is further enhanced with the provision of only three high and narrow lancet windows provided with shutters, some 2.2m above ground level. The tower of two storeys was originally entered from a narrow, barred doorway from the nave with a newel staircase built into the thickness of the south-east corner. The first floor contains a fireplace, the flue of which passes through a projecting turret on the south side of the battlemented parapet. Tunnel vaulting over the ground floor and a nave roof of stone flags provide further protection. A doorway in the eastern wall of the second storey of the tower, now blocked, suggests that there may have been an attic refuge room.

# The pele towers

A new form of ecclesiastical fortification was developed in the marches and remained confined to the north of England. Built to protect the village priest and occasionally priors, the remains of fourteen vicars' pele towers and four for priors are found between Carlisle and Newcastle.[8] The vicar's pele built in the English Eastern March, in the small town of Corbridge east of Hexham in Northumberland, is of particular interest. It was built in St Andrew's churchyard in the early fourteenth century in response to the destructive Scottish raids of 1296, 1311 and 1313. Although partially ruined it demonstrates the way these towers, intended for clerical occupation, were fortified. The tower is of three storeys measuring 11m to the crenellations of the fighting platform, and has a steeply pitched roof; some of the merlons are preserved. Each corner of the platform was provided with square corner turrets or bartizans resting on corbels with machicolations, now much ruined. Entry to the rectangular tower, measuring 8 x 6m, is through a narrow arched doorway in the north-eastern corner holding a double-planked door reinforced with bands of iron and a draw bar. It opens into the barrel-vaulted ground-floor basement provided with an archer's loop-hole in the southern and western wall; the straight, narrow staircase runs in the thickness of the eastern wall to the first floor of the tower. This was the living room of the incumbent and is not only spacious, measuring 5.4 x 3.8m, but is provided with a garderobe, a fireplace, a washroom with a stone table and sink and niches in the walls for books. Splayed windows in the north and south walls are provided with benches. In spite of the narrowness of the windows and the solitary loop-hole, it is surprisingly light and airy; a book rest near to the small window in the west wall is so positioned as to gain maximum lighting from the northern winter sun. Stairs run again in the thickness of the east wall to reach the top-floor bedroom; spartan in comparison with the living room it too is well lit. Access to the fighting platform is by means of a wooden ladder from an ante-room in the thickness of the eastern wall.

Examination of the nearby church, part of which is of pre-Norman date, reveals no direct evidence of any active defences and it appears that the vicar's pele stood alone as a defensive tower. So far little attention has been paid concerning the role these towers played. Certainly the clergy were threatened by the Scots, but so were the rest of the inhabitants of this small

---

[8] The term pele is somewhat contentious. Believed to originate from palisade, it has come to denote a solitary fortified tower in the north of England.

# The VICAR'S PELE
## The Parish Church of St. Andrew
## CORBRIDGE Northumberland

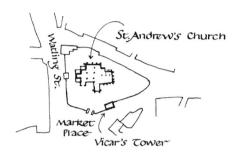

Watling St.

St. Andrew's Church

Market Place

Vicar's Tower

10 R 96

Battlements

Top Floor

First Floor

Ground Floor

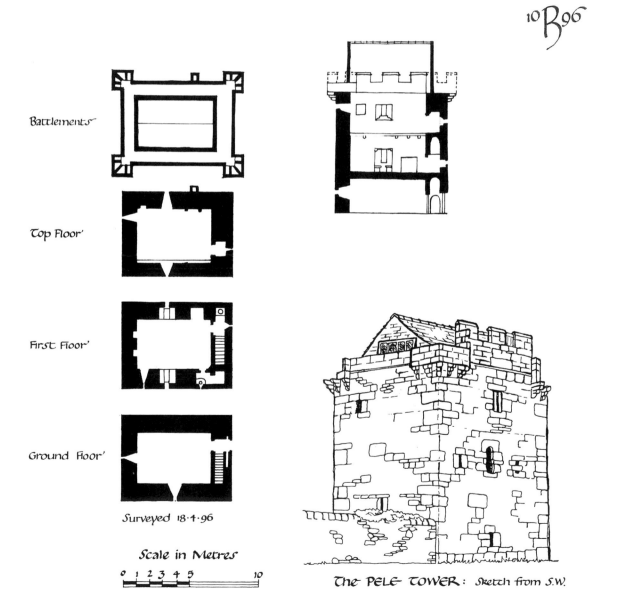

Surveyed 18·4·96

Scale in Metres

0 1 2 3 4 5 10

THE PELE TOWER : Sketch from S.W.

its full height, more or less intact. Built of brick and stone, the central three-storey gatehouse of the fourteenth century is flanked either side by plain brick walls containing loop-holed galleries terminating in southern and northern slim, loop-holed cylindrical towers adjoining the brick precinct walls. The abbot was given permission to crenellate in 1382 and the façade is a curious mixture of decorative loops for cross bows and saintly statuary; it also served as the lodgings of the abbot. Above the main entrance are three statues representing the Virgin, the patroness of the abbey, St John the Baptist to her left and an unknown bishop on her right. There is documentary evidence that the battlemented parapet was embellished with statues. These were of soldiers, brandishing swords and pole-arms, all overlooking the entrance gate. It towered above the brick-built defensive enclosure wall that was further protected by moats and a lake. Although much adorned and decorated the gatehouse and abbot's lodging could offer serious defence but to whom is uncertain. It was built at a time of peasant unrest and when French and Scottish pirates were active. The recorded history is uneventful and it appears that the gatehouse defences were never tested. Intriguingly, a brick-built barbican was constructed across the western moat in the sixteenth century. Strangely set at an angle of almost 70 degrees to the gate façade, it runs for 38m and terminates in two round towers. It contains gun-loops as well as those for cross bows, and, somewhat bizarrely, a garderobe.

The most powerful of all ecclesiastical fortifications are, however, to be found at the coastal priory of **Tynemouth**, north of Newcastle, built on a prominent headland. The defensible nature of the site had been recognised before the founding of the priory and there were fortifications here before the priory was given licence to crenellate in 1296, long after the priory had been built. Of the fortification built by the priors, the gatehouse with its barbican and the mediaeval wall running all round the headland remain; most defences are, however, from later periods. Earthworks, dug across the headland reveted in stone, are Elizabethan, contemporary with the defences of Berwick to the north. Over the ensuing centuries it was constantly updated as a coastal artillery fortress and served as such through the Napoleonic and First and Second World Wars, finally losing its guns in 1956.

## Summary

Britain has the remains of a considerable number of ecclesiastical fortifications, one of which, the vicar's pele, is only found in the north of England. Almost all the recognised fortified religious buildings are found in the marches but much work needs to be done in Yorkshire, the Anglo-Welsh borders and south Wales to understand the extent to which churches, in particular, were fortified and used as refuges. The round tower churches of East Anglia have not been included as it seems highly unlikely that they had a defensive role. For a similar reason Saxon towers have been excluded.

A number of monasteries were fortified on the south coast, especially during the Hundred Years War, for protection against the French navy, but not as part of any coastal defensive scheme.[25]

There are a number of ecclesiastical fortifications in the hinterland of England that were

[25] The solitary exception is at Tynemouth, which became part of Henry VIII's coastal defence scheme.

fortified, usually in response to localised situations. Bishop Ralph of Shrewsbury, during his quarrel with the city, built the walls, gatehouse and moat of his palace at Wells in Somerset and the great gatehouse at Bury St Edmunds was built to counter threats posed to the abbots by the townsfolk.

Apart from the Anglo-Scottish Borders, however, the need to fortify ecclesiastic buildings had ended by the fifteenth century. A number of churches were nonetheless pressed into service during the English Civil War (e.g. Clun), which was used as a strong point, and at Bradford, where the cathedral was protected by bales of wool.

# BEAUMONT-du-PÉRIGORD

### Bastide founded by Edward I in 1272

### Dordogne
### FRANCE

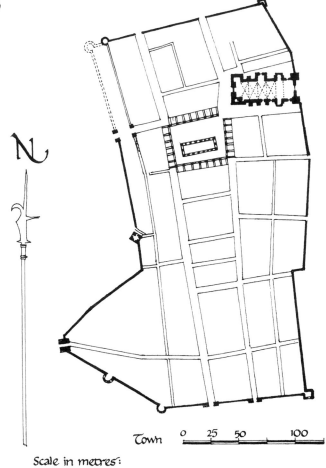

N

| Town | 0 | 25 | 50 | 100 |

Scale in metres:

| Church | 0 | 5 | 10 | 25 |

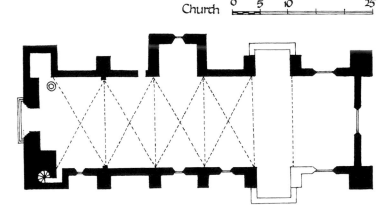

Gothic fortified church of St Laurent and St Front c. early 14th

a staircase to the first floor, ladders subsequently providing access to the chemin de ronde and the fighting platform of the tower, which is roofed, crenellated and built on projecting machicolations. A flight of stairs, in the nave by the west wall, leads down to a well: a further indication that the citizenry regarded their church as serving as the town citadel.

The chevets of other churches form part of the town walls at **Sauveterre-d'Aveyron**, **Fleurance**, **Monflanquin** and **Saint-Pastour**, whilst the south wall of the churches of **Montréal** and **Miradoux** form part of the town ramparts.

There is no formal arrangement between the fortified church of a bastide and any other fortifications that it may have. At **Molières**, near Bergerac in the Dordogne, a small English bastide was established at an important crossroads in 1284. Only the Gothic church, set a little off the regular line of houses and near the town square, received fortifications, with solid nave and chancel walls. The western, solitary and narrow doorway was fortified with the addition of two massive square towers originally connected by a crenellated gallery. The church was damaged in the Wars of Religion and has been substantially rebuilt. The side walls of the church and the north tower remain from the thirteenth century and show just how big and powerful this church was, far bigger than would have been required for religious purposes. It contained store-rooms and could accommodate the whole population of the bastide, which never exceeded 1200.[16]

Other fortified churches lie free-standing within the town defences. At **Beaumont-de-Lomagne** the fourteenth-century church occupies an insula near the market place. Its considerable bulk was fortified with a machicolated chemin de ronde, corner towers and a crenellated fighting gallery on the bell-tower. The twelfth-century church at **Vianne** had been included within the enceinte of the bastide founded by Edward I in 1284 on his Agenais frontier, opposite the French town of Lavardac. Overlooking the north gate the church was actively fortified with a tall crenellated bell-tower.

These fortified bastide churches demonstrate a close co-operation between the Church and the laity, the king, the founder and the townspeople, whereby substantial economies of expenditure and labour could be made in producing buildings which served temporal as well as spiritual needs.

# The fortified rural parish churches of the south and west of France and the 'scourge of God'

The stimulus to fortify remote and often isolated rural parish churches in France was the war that developed between England and France. It began in 1337 when Edward III claimed the throne of France and continued until 1453 when the English finally lost Bordeaux. In the interval the rural peasantry had to contend not only with the depredations of the warring factions but also with the Great Plague and famine. Although some protection was offered by the bastides, the rural hamlets and villages had to fend for themselves, and it was the nature of warfare during this Hundred Years War that resulted in the fortification of probably thousands

---

[16] A start was made in 1314 to build a castle keep to the north of the town but it was never completed.

of churches. Although it was an intermittent war with few pitched battles, it affected every aspect of life in both the English and French regions. Whilst the main impact and consequences were felt in north-eastern France, where the English armies invaded via Calais and its Pale, and the south and south-west, where English possessions in Aquitaine were used to launch raids and invasions, other areas were not free of warfare. Using the conflict as an excuse, many of the nobility in other regions took the opportunity to settle feuds.[17] The agrarian peasantry was greatly affected on two counts; for decades they had to strive for survival when food was scarce and cope with warfare. In the main, English armies were small, rarely numbering more than a few thousand unless a major expedition was led by the king. It was instead the activities and tactics of the grand or free companies and the routiers that was to have such a devastating effect.

The English invented the chevauchée, literally a ride or cavalcade, wherein bands of mercenary soldiers, all seasoned veterans, banded together under a captain to undertake rapacious raids into enemy territory.[18] More frequent, however, were lightning hit-and-run tactics of the smaller free companies of professional soldiers. Whilst these soldiers came from all over Europe they were usually led by English captains, many of whom amassed substantial fortunes. The virulence and violence of these raids led to tremendous fear amongst the suffering civil population. The free companies gained a reputation as the 'scourge of God'.

The countryside could only provide so much booty, however, and there were significant periods when the soldiery were confined to garrison duty or disbanded. Many then joined lawless bands, preferring a life of pillage and freedom to one of poverty and serfdom. These bands installed themselves in minor castles and forts and systematically reduced the surrounding countryside to desolation. Once installed, the routiers were difficult to dislodge.

French peasant response was first directed towards survival by any means.[19] They faced stark choices. They could submit and become destitute, frequently losing their lives; they could flee to the dense forests then covering much of France, taking with them what they could; they could seek shelter in the larger towns or seigneurial castles until danger had passed; or they could defend themselves, either passively or actively.

## The fortifications of the rural population

English armies and garrisons were never very large and those communities that decided to try to defend themselves against the depredations of the avaricious soldiery had to find the will and resources to do so. The larger fortified towns and castles were safe from English attack. It was the smaller towns, villages, hamlets, farming communities and the rural monasteries and

---

[17] Curry and Hughes (1994: 103–14).

[18] Some idea of the nature and consequences of such a raid is given by the Great Chevauchée led by Edward the Black Prince. Comprising a great company of mounted archers and men-at-arms, it left Bordeaux in October 1355 and in the space of two months reached Narbonne in the Languedoc, a distance of 900km. The sole aim was to capture, plunder and destroy towns and villages along the way. Such a chevauchée became known as a route and the participating soldiers as routiers.

[19] Wright gives a good insight in the relationship between soldier and peasant in the Hundred Years War.

priories that were most at risk, and it was here that fortification in earnest began in those regions at risk.

Rural villages and hamlets rarely had a building of any size that could be fortified, with the exception of the church – often a substantial stone building with a bell-tower. It could be economically adapted for defence in a variety of ways, sometimes speedily and within the resources of the populace. The numbers that remain demonstrate the popularity and necessity of such fortifications. Equally they may indicate that there was no alternative and any defence was better than none.

## The manner of church fortifications

A papal bull of 1059 had offered protection to churches, their cemeteries for a distance of thirty paces in all directions, and other consecrated ground, by the threat of excommunication. Although revived in the twelfth century, it had ceased to offer much protection against the routiers and lawless bands that roamed through much of France in the fourteenth and fifteenth centuries. Spiritual defence needed to be augmented by a pragmatic approach of using the church to provide a safe refuge. When a community decided to fortify its church permission was required from royal, ecclesiastical or municipal authorities.[20]

Many factors influenced the fortification of a church, not least the resources of the parish community. Examination of extant examples shows that there was a huge variation in the degree, style and combinations of defensive features; in addition regional variations produced differing military architectural styles. Perhaps the most common way a church was adapted for refuge and defence was by the elevation of the walls and roof to provide rooms for shelter and active defence above the ceilings of the nave and chancel. These rooms could be loopholed, or provided with box machicolations to produce a salle de défense. As well as protecting the villagers, their chattels, provisions, animals and implements when attacked some churches provided in their elevated refuges rooms to be occupied by village families at night, when there was significant real or perceived threat. They were rented for generations. The church of **St Radegoude** in Rouergue is one such example, where in addition to the elevation of the nave and chancel the side chapels of the transepts were converted into multi-storey defence towers. The salle de refuge contains some forty rooms for parish families, two of which contain fireplaces, almost certainly for the village captain and the parish priest. In some of the larger churches a covered, crenellated gallery would run all round the church, chevet, choir, transepts, nave and western façade, thus enabling defenders to have easy access to any part of the church defences. Where the church had an attached tower its summit would be provided with a crenellated parapet or received a wooden hoard. The intervening storeys were sometimes provided with fireplaces, chimneys and garderobes. The towers were used for lookout and the bells to signal a warning. The simple hoarding around the top of the tower was replaced by more sophisticated machicolations on corbels. The earlier arch machicolations that first

---

[20] Unlicensed or adulterine fortifications were subject to debate by church councils, who felt that such defences were open to abuse, and a number of statutes were issued prohibiting such building works and functional alterations.

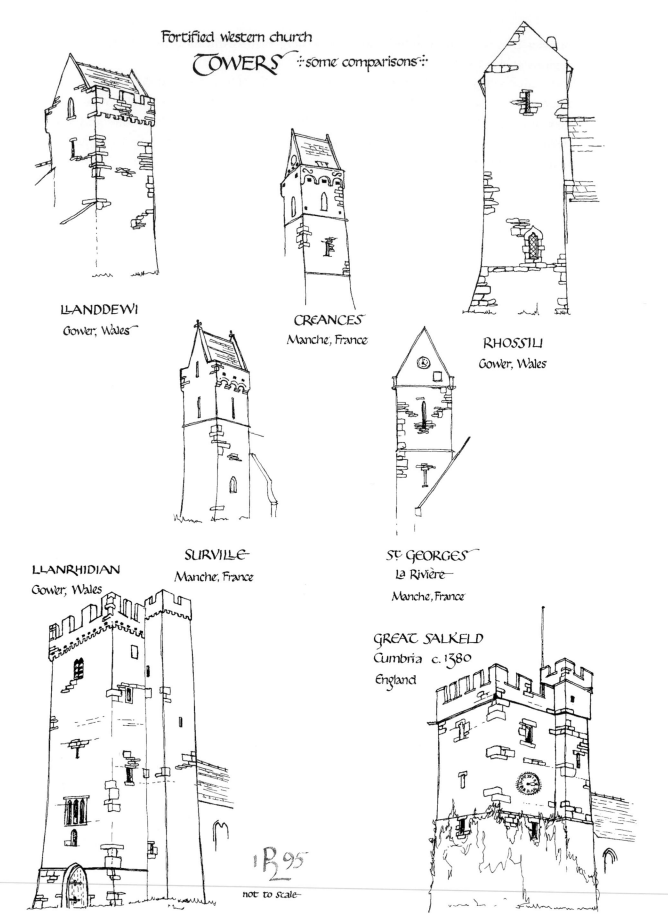

Fortified western church

**TOWERS** ∴ some comparisons ∴

LLANDDEWI
Gower, Wales

CREANCES
Manche, France

RHOSSILI
Gower, Wales

SURVILLE
Manche, France

ST GEORGES
La Rivière
Manche, France

LLANRHIDIAN
Gower, Wales

GREAT SALKELD
Cumbria c. 1380
England

IB 95

not to scale

appeared on the coastal churches of Provence were built well into the fifteenth century.

The various openings in the walls of the church were fortified and defended in a variety of ways. The doors themselves were usually of double-planked oak clamped together with iron bolts and sheathed with iron plates to protect against axe and flame. One or more draw bars further strengthened the door against battering. When the entrance was via the western façade it was frequently defended by a crenellated and machicolated gallery running between defence towers placed at the southern and northern angles of the façade. In other instances a box machicolation or bretache overlooked the door. There are, rarely, remains of grooves for a raised drawbridge or portcullis and archival evidence of a barbican. In some instances the inside door to the nave from a porch entrance would be overlooked by a similar structure to a bretache, known as an assommoir.

Windows would be bricked up, defended by stout iron bars and grilles often overlooked by a bretache and shuttered from the inside. Loopholed towers, both square and round, were added onto the church in a variety of ways, and frequently smaller round towers or echauguettes were built at the corners of the church. They were usually corbelled out from the buttresses and are found at the west end of the nave, on transepts and occasionally at the chancel end.

The church at **Saint-Pierrevillers**, near Spincourt in Meuse, still has most of its fortifications and shows the sophisticated way in which a simple parish church was transformed into a maison-fort, the stronghouse of a farming community. Perched upon a grassy knoll in the centre of a farming hamlet the original church consisted of a simple western tower, nave and chancel. Some time in the fifteenth century it was totally remodelled to protect its parishioners. The nave, probably in response to an increase in population, was remodelled in 1530, and the chancel heightened to provide a defence room containing loopholes and box machicolations also loopholed for firearms. Sixteen bretaches were placed to overlook every opening of the church, be it door, window or defence opening. The roof of both nave and chancel was stone-vaulted with meuretières at the rib crossings providing observation of the body of the church. Both sides of the narrow tower were boxed in to run flush with the nave walls and to provide a fortified western façade. Entry to the church was by a single doorway in the northern wall of the nave with its fortified door.[21] The defence rooms were reached by means of the northern extension to the tower that contains a wooden spiral staircase, where, however, the bottom six steps are stone. At the side of the door to the staircase is a gun-loop covering the nave and the entrance to the church. Thus anybody breaking into the church would be subjected to fire from the salle de défense and the staircase tower. A cemetery wall surrounds the church, still to a height of 2m, and the bretaches are so arranged that they cover both churchyard and all approaches from the hamlet.

Some villages were fortified with walls and towers, with the fortified church forming part of the enceinte. Partially ruined, the walled village of **Cruas** in Ardèche crowns a promontory dominating the Rhône valley. The roughly quadrangular enceinte dates from the fourteenth century and is reinforced with rectangular towers to the north, east and south. Steep sides

---

[21] When first visited in 1992, the double-planked and studded door still contained half of its iron sheathing. At a repeat visit a decade later the door had been repaired and all traces of its iron façade removed.

further protect the northern and southern approaches. Found on the vulnerable western boundary of the village the church was converted into a huge donjon with the addition of two loopholed storeys, corner towers and a fighting platform with arch machicolations. Outwardly it has the stark appearance of a rectangular keep. The walled village contains the remains of approximately sixty buildings, suggesting a population of around three hundred, although there were probably village houses outside the walls.

At **Rudelle**, near Figerac in Lot, there is a similar church donjon standing in isolation of any other fortifications. Here the twelfth-century Romanesque church was elevated with the addition of two storeys of a purely military form. The crenellated fighting platform also contains projecting bretaches overlooking the western entrance doorway and the narrow lancet windows of the ground floor church. The middle storey contains only cruciform arrow loops. Both church donjons are similar to that built at Safita in the Holy Land.

In other instances the central fortified church was surrounded on all four sides with contiguous housing, whose outer walls, pierced only by narrow and high windows, provided a first line of defence. **Brigueil** in Charente is fortified in this way. Built on a knoll, the central church of Saint-Martial received fortifications from the twelfth to the sixteenth centuries; it has a crenellated salle de défense and a bell-tower containing gun-loops, although the church underwent restoration in the nineteenth century when many defensive features were lost. Although the external blank walls of the surrounding houses formed part of the enceinte the two entrance gateways were reinforced by drum towers and a portcullis. The defences were not sufficient to resist a besieging English army in 1356, however.

Whether fortified or not, churches were on occasion protected by a defensive cemetery wall. The small Alsatian village of **Hunawihr**, in Haut-Rhin near Ribeauville, is set amongst rolling vineyards and is overlooked to the north by its church encircled by a cemetery wall. Although the church is of a later date – nave and tower are from the fifteenth and sixteenth centuries – the polygonal fortified cemetery wall dates from the twelfth century and has been kept in a good state of repair. Reinforced by six open-backed semi-circular flanking towers, the wall is 1m thick and today is devoid of battlements. Equipped with archery loopholes, some of which have been adapted for use by handguns, the enceinte is entered from the north via a simple gatehouse provided with embrasures for small cannon. Although a number of churches were defended by cemetery walls in Alsace, the churches themselves were not fortified; this is in contrast to neighbouring Lorraine where both church and cemetery were fortified.

In the Ariège region of the Midi-Pyreneés, the church of the small village of **Seintein** remains surrounded by a fortified cemetery wall. Extending for 200m, it still retains three of the original six four-storey towers that defended the churchyard; altered over the centuries, the fortified appearance is still very striking. Although fortified cemetery walls are found throughout the country, the great majority that still exist, in varying states of disrepair, are to be found in the north and east of France. Many have been demolished and the numbers can only be guessed at.

Churches continued to be designed and built as fortresses until the seventeenth century. Built in 1624 by the villagers, with the help of Claude de Joyeuse, count of Grande, the church of **Saint-Juvin**, near Vouziers in the Ardennes, is one such church. Situated in the centre of the village on a small knoll, the rectangular church measures 32 x 16.5m. It was built to shelter the villagers and contains a well and storage cellars for provisions. The western façade has a bretache over the entrance and contains three tiers of gun-loops between the circular echauguettes built on top of the rectangular corner buttresses. Stairways in both sides of this façade lead to the towers and the chemin de ronde that ran all round the church under the eaves. The chevet is similarly defended, although the echauguettes are pentangular and rest on corbels. Both the northern and southern walls of the nave have a row of gun-loops from the chemin de ronde running under the eaves. The southern doorway is overlooked by a bretache. Although the narrow lancet windows of the north wall appear original, the windows in the south look like replacements, possibly from when the church interior was restored after the First World War. The brick vaulting, supported by stone rib vaults branching from ten piers in the twin-aisled nave, is roofed with slates. Dominating the village, the church is in reality a powerful peasant fort capable of providing shelter and a stout defence for large numbers of villagers.

# Souterrains

A number of churches were provided with souterrains by their parishioners, entered from either the cemetery or the church itself. These underground refuge rooms connected by tunnels vary in extent, some running underground for up to 100m, and contain an average of five rooms. It is postulated that the spoil from their construction was used in building the church or its defences. Endeavours were made to camouflage the entrance, always located in a well-defended part of the church or cemetery. They further demonstrate the insecurity of peasants in many parts of the country and the efforts and resources that some parish populations put into defending themselves.

The entrance gallery runs steeply downwards and requires any entrant to stoop. This gallery led to a central passageway from which the refuge rooms were excavated. It was defended in two ways. Firstly, at the bottom of the entrance gallery a deep pit with steep sides was cut down into the rock, into which the unwary fell. Steep sides made climbing out difficult. This pit was overlooked by a spy hole from a small guard-room and a loophole was strategically inserted, through which a pike could despatch any attacker thus trapped. Secondly, the entrance into the refuge itself was protected by a thick door fastened flush with the rim of the pit, which would be closed and barred once the wooden bridge used by the villages to cross the pit had been retracted into the souterrain. Walls of logs inserted into rebates in the passageways provided further obstacles to any intruders. Once inside the individual refuge rooms could only be entered from very narrow tunnels, or gulots, through which the occupants had to wriggle. Rarely more than 50cm in diameter and around 1.5m long, they sloped downwards so that anyone crawling through had to put both arms on the ground and was thus unable to protect himself against a defender. The refuge rooms were aerated by means of carefully designed ventilation shafts, which, like the escape exit, were carefully disguised where they emerged on the surface.[22]

[22] Triolet and Triolet (1995: 81–9) describe in detail souterrains in France. Interestingly, of the six examples of these underground refuge rooms which are entered from a church or its cemetery yard, only one, at Compreignac in Haute-Vienne, is mentioned by Salch.

The souterrain had a number of distinct advantages. The dark and disorientating passages produced an environment of fear, especially when the pit-trap and probing pike were encounted. The barking of ferocious guard dogs would similarly act as a deterrent. Designed to be the last place of refuge, entered if the church was about to fall to attackers, souterrains provided an excellent deterrent to roving bands, who would, hopefully, go in search of easier pickings. Even if the disguised entrance or exit was discovered access was all but impossible for any assailant.

There was the added advantage that, unlike many temporary village and church fortifications that were dismantled on the orders of the clergy or local nobility when danger had passed, once built they were permanent. Although there are many examples of souterrains under towns, villages and castles in France, the number that were added to churches will remain unknown. Most new discoveries have been accidental.

The souterrain at **Petosse** in Vendée follows the classic form. It was built towards the end of the sixteenth century. It is now entered from the nave, but the original entrance was from the cemetery. As approximately half of the refuge rooms lie under the floor of the cruciform church it was probably constructed when the church was rebuilt following the sacking by the Calvinists in 1562. Running downwards, it leads to the pit-trap overlooked by a guard-room. From the central gallery at least three cruciate refuge rooms are reached after passing through gulots. Each wing measures approximately 5 x 2m and is excavated to allow the occupants to stand. Niches for lamps are provided, together with benches. The whole complex extends for approximately 100m under both church and cemetery.

# Regional variations

France has a rich heritage of churches which like their counterparts elsewhere have been much damaged, altered, rebuilt or restored over the centuries. The attempt to classify regional variations is limited to churches that still today show evidence of fortifications and where photographic and pictorial archival material is strong. In addition there is often an overlap of styles from region to region and some specific features occur only in a few churches, often found close together.

# Northern France

### Normandy

All of the fortified churches have tall bell-towers, usually fortified with a crenellated parapet on false machicolations and often with a saddle-back roof to the tower as at **Créance** and **Surville**. Built of rough coursed granite, they are austere and functional with minimal decoration or embellishment. Found mainly in coastal regions and particularly in the Cotentin peninsula, they sheltered their parishioners from the piratical raids of the Hundred Years War.[23] The most impressive is found at **Portbail** near Barneville-Carteret. Here the twelfth-century

---

[23] There is some similarity between them and certain churches in Gower in south Wales, although no connection can be made.

Romanesque chapel of Saint-Nicholas-de-Pierrepont had attached to its south-eastern aspect, in the fifteenth century, an enormous five-storey fortified bell-tower crowned with a crenellated fighting platform on blind arcades. It was the lookout tower, and part of the harbour defences of this small port.

## Aisne

Fortified churches are widespread in this north-eastern frontier of France and the most impressive are to be found in **La Thiérache**, an area of the region that lies between the Rivers Oise and Serre, that contains sixty-eight fortified churches whose defences date mainly from 1550–1650. Meuret has described three distinct architectural styles. Some churches were only altered in appearance by the addition of active defensive features, including the heightening of the nave or chancel, the addition of echauguettes on corner buttresses and the provision of loopholes and bretaches. The basic structure of the church is easily recognised and good examples are found at **Morgny-en-Thiérache** and at **Moncornet**. Here the Gothic stone-built cruciform church of the thirteenth century, built in the centre of the small town, was fortified in the sixteenth century by its inhabitants. The western porch, flanked by two tall cylindrical towers containing tiers of loopholes, was overlooked by a fortified platform that ran between the towers and contained meuretières. The lower half is built of stone and embrasures for small cannon overlook the entrance steps. A plaque commemorating the builders dates the work to 1546–7. Each angle of the transept and of the choir carried a loopholed echaugette. Overlooking the partial blocked window of the chevet is a bretache and the row of loopholes under the eaves indicates the presence of a chemin de ronde or salle de défense. As well as providing efficient protection for the townsfolk, the church is also an expression of the prosperity of the town.

The church at **Englancourt** dominates the valley of the Oise and also received its fortifications in the sixteenth century. The rectangular stone-built Romanesque church, measuring 25 x 7m had two brick echauguettes added to the western entrance to the nave, provided with loopholes to cover the entrance. It is very similar to the façade of the church of **Marly Gomont** on the opposite side of the valley. The nave was elevated, also in brick, to provide a salle de refuge, but it was the choir that received the greater part of the fortifications. The chancel was almost completely rebuilt in brick to produce a large square tower, rib-vaulted and provided with two corner towers at each end of the flat chevet, both of which contain four tiers of loopholes that covered all aspects of the church, other than the western end. The square salle de refuge above the vaulting of the choir has few external openings and is reached by a narrow, easily defended staircase within the thickness of the wall. These were counted as fortified churches by Meuret.

Fewer in number are his donjon or fort churches. Here the earlier Romanesque or Gothic church has vast brick, and usually square, towers attached to the western end of the church, out of all proportion with and totally dominating the church and village houses. These towers are purely military in design and function and were immense undertakings. **Prisces, Saint-Martin-de-Jeantes** and **Burelles** are amongst the finest examples of this group of twenty-four churches. Built in the middle of a small farming hamlet, Prisces has a Romanesque nave and choir of the twelfth century. Stone-built, it is devoid of all traces of fortification, although a monastery was already fortified by 1356 with the Romanesque monastic church and bell-tower being defended by a crenellated and machicolated parapet. The monastic close was walled, and the southern gateway, placed between two round towers, contained a drawbridge. Following the defeat of King Jean II le Bon by the Black Prince at the Battle of Poitiers in 1356, the monastery was sacked and the defences slighted by the English. It was not until the end of the fifteenth century that the monastery was refortified, to be followed by a hundred years of prosperity before the Wars of Religion broke out, which were pursued with a particular virulence in the area. Led by Admiral Coligny, Protestant troops attacked the monastery in 1569, pillaged its treasures and set alight both ecclesiastical and secular buildings. It was nearly eighty years before reconstruction began and the chancel, roof, and dormitories date from this period. A seventeenth-century print in the church shows the monastery restored to its former glory. The defences that have survived are those remaining from the fifteenth century with the addition of the fortified abbot's lodgings in the north-west corner of the monastic enclosure and a new entrance in the north-east.

**Mont-Saint-Michel**, in Manche, is not only a famous pilgrimage site but also one of the best-known ecclesiastical complexes in Western Europe.[26] Now one of France's most popular tourist attractions, its imposing situation on a huge rock in the bay of the same name is somewhat different from when it was fortified after the start of the Hundred Years War. Much of the bay has become silted up over the centuries and a causeway from the mainland was constructed in the nineteenth century, whilst the original Romanesque abbey and its attendant Gothic claustral buildings have undergone significant changes. The defences have remained the same, however.

In 1357 the abbots were made titular captains of the garrison, which lodged in the village straddling the southeastern face of the rock, and began their fortification against the English. The abbey was fortified and made impregnable (except at its eastern entrance) with the construction of the Châtelet, completed in 1393; it is a powerful combination of twin towers, machicolations, barbican, a guardhouse and steep steps. Despite the purely military nature of these defences the use of pink and grey stone enables it to harmonise with the monastic church. The importance of the Mount and its symbolic value to the French was not lost on the abbots and they spent considerable sums on building huge cisterns under the flags of the nave, chancel, crypt and almonry in case of being cut off from the mainland. Fed by an intricate system of rainwater channels and a filtration system, they provided water supplies for the Mount and its inhabitants until very recently. Considered too steep to assail, even if soldiers could be landed on the rocky shore, the northern part of the rock remained unfortified, although the rest of the shoreline received powerful defences to protect the village and southern approaches to the monastery. Dating from the fourteenth century, they proved successful in resisting many English attempts to storm the Mount. Helped by the citizens of St

---

[26] The cult of the Archangel Michael, one of the warrior saints, arrived in Europe from the East. Believed to be the champion of the forces of good over evil, and the dispenser of justice, his abbey received many pilgrims throughout the Hundred Years War. Although the English frequently isolated the Mount from the mainland their entrepreneurial instincts allowed pilgrims to cross on payment of a fee.

Malo and a garrison of knights, it remained French throughout the Hundred Years War. The heroic defence of the abbey and islet by Louis d'Estoutville and his hundred and nineteen knights in 1425 was to become a symbol of French resistance.[27] Viollet-le-Duc when he visited the Mount in 1835 thought that 'No place could be more beautiful or savage, nowhere more grandiose or melancholy'.[28]

Of all the fortified ecclesiastical buildings in France the **Palace of the Popes** in Avignon remains the most powerful statement of ecclesiastical might both in its symbolism and in the strength of its fortifications. Although only occupied by the popes for forty-three years until Gregory XI took the papacy back to Rome in 1377 it is a monumental ensemble of two fortresses built next to each other by two successive popes during a period of eighteen years. Today they remain much as they were when first built, although further additions and alterations were made by a number of succeeding papal legates.[29]

The first papal fortress, the Old Palace, was built as a symbol of pontifical power and to protect the pope, church treasures and archives from feuding nobility and opportunistic brigands. Started in 1334 by the Cistercian Pope Benedict XII it took just eight years to build. Modelled on the Cistercian monastic plan, with the addition of fortifications on a massive scale, the quadrangular Tour Trouillas, measuring 20 x 17m and rising to a height of 50m, dominates the fortress from the north-east corner of the fortified cloister. Crowned by a crenellated parapet with machicolations supported by corbels, this is powerful military architecture. The cloister was fortified in the manner of the monastery churches to the south with a chemin de ronde running on arch machicolations between buttresses. The eastern cloister with its attached consistory was extended to the south to include the first defensive tower erected, that of the Tower of Angels.

This extension was incorporated by Clement VI (1352–62) when he added the New Palace, an altogether different building. Using as his architect Jean du Louvres, he added two further wings. The first ran westwards from the Tower of Angels and enclosed the great audience chamber with the Chapel of Clementine above: the second ran from the western end of this wing northwards to join the south-west corner of the Old Palace, thus enclosing the Grand Courtyard. The altogether softer façade of the New Palace reflects the difference between the austere Cistercians and the more exuberant Benedictines. The end result was two palaces forming one monumental building constructed of fine white Burgundian ashlar. It was described by the mediaeval chronicler Froissart as the 'strongest and most beautiful in the world'. Of particular interest is the latrine tower that may have been a forerunner of the Dansker towers of the Teutonic Knights. It encroached on the north-eastern tower of Trouillas but was separate from the living quarters. Two storeys connected to two of the cloister galleries were exclusively latrines. The upper latrines occupied the whole floor, while the lower occupied

---

[27] Braunfels (1972: 187).

[28] Le-Duc was a nineteenth-century mediaevalist who oversaw the rebuilding of many mediaeval ruins. His monument is the restored walled southern city of Carcassonne. By the time of his visit the Mount had become a prison, and this combined with the inclement weather of March suggest factors other than the architecture may have influenced his opinion.

[29] It was restored in the nineteenth century by Viollet-le-Duc along with the city walls.

present site in 1334–5 by Dragovol Hrelyo. It was repeatedly attacked by the Turks, particularly in the fifteenth and sixteenth centuries, and only the defence tower remains from the Middle Ages.

The site chosen for the monastery is impressive; it lies in an isolated position above the fertile valley of the River Riska and below the beech and pine forests cladding the Rila Mountains. The four walls of the monastery, almost rhomboidal in shape, built out of granite and with a patchy coat of whitewash, appear at first sight austere and fortress-like. The presence of so many windows would undermine any defensive role, however. Based on the Athonite plan, the central church is surrounded by storey upon storey of monastic cells and rooms. There is a departure, however, from monastic design, one not seen anywhere else in Bulgaria. In the centre of the monastic courtyard is the huge fourteenth-century Hrelyo Tower, the sole surviving building from before the nineteenth-century rebuilding.[18] Rising, in five storeys above its basement to a height of 23m, it is rectangular in shape, measuring 8.25 x 7.75m. Built of well-coursed granite and sandstone rubble, three buttresses on each side are joined below the uppermost storey by semi-circular brick-built arches resulting in arch machicolations. The top storey contains the chapel of the tower and is gently domed. Surrounding the chapel is a fighting gallery incorporating the arch machicolations. Both the chapel and gallery roofs are battlemented to provide, in addition, a fighting platform. Entrance is from the first storey and the staircase runs clockwise in the thickness of the walls to the chapel. An impressive fortification, with few loopholes to light individual storeys, it stands, incongruous, amongst the ornate and seemingly luxurious monastic buildings of five hundred years later.

Although there remains little evidence of fortification in most of Bulgaria's seventy-six monasteries, many played a vital role in the attainment of Bulgarian independence. Writers, plotters and revolutionary leaders were sheltered and protected; the monastery at **Etropole** for example sheltered, for a considerable time, Vassil Levski, Bulgaria's 'Apostle of Freedom', in a specially built hideout.

The situation in Serbia was somewhat different; many powerful fortifications remain from the Middle Ages, and suggest that considerable resources were used in the defence of many of its monasteries. The turbulent history of Serbia, and its frequent role as a battleground between Habsburg Austria and the Ottoman Turks has resulted in the ruination and dismantling of many monastic fortified enceintes.

Monumental remains of its fortifications remain at the monastery of **Manasija**, demonstrating how mediaeval Serbia fashioned monastery and castle as one. Dedicated to the Holy Trinity, it was founded by the despot Stephan Lazarevic at a time when the Turks were threatening Serbia. It soon became enveloped in the massive fortifications that remain today in an almost intact state. The architecturally complex church is dwarfed by the mediaeval enceinte, reinforced by eleven towers. Eight are rectangular, one serving as the keep, while one is square and two hexagonal. Originally moated, the defences were not sufficient to prevent

---

[18] Whether it was built in the centre of the original monastery is unknown. Careful examination of this unique defensive tower does not reveal any evidence to suggest that it has ever been attached to or bonded with any other building.

capture by the Turks in 1439. Despoiled by them in 1456, it was recaptured along with the rest of northern Serbia by the Habsburgs in 1718. Although the powder store, kept in the narthex by the Austrians, blew up in 1735, the church still retains many of its early frescoes, including some of the warrior saints armed in the manner of the Serbian knights of the fifteenth century. The church was further damaged in 1804 just before the Serbian uprising, but has subsequently been restored. Of the other monasteries that received a similar enceinte none remain as complete as at Manasija.

Although the Dalmatian coast had been prey to the Ottoman navy and Saracen corsairs, the Battle of Lepanto in 1571 effectively broke any naval supremacy they had in the central Mediterranean, and much of the Adriatic remained safe for Venetian shipping. Isolated settlements were, however, still at risk from raiders, especially the fierce Uskok pirates who used the Croatian port of Split as their base. Allying themselves with the populations of the islands of Hvar and Brac, in the sixteenth century they supported both Turks and Venetians, depending on the way the conflict was going. In addition, they were not averse to opportunistic freebooting, and many coastal settlements and island towns along the Dalmatian Coast became extensively fortified.

Churches and monasteries were not immune. On the Croatian island of **Mljet**, the Benedictine monks, despite the protection of Venice and the Republic of Ragusa in Dubrovnik, thought it prudent to fortify their monastery and church of St Mary, despite its isolated position on a rocky islet in a sea loch. Although much of the islet would be difficult to assault because of its rocky nature, the western half, containing the monastic buildings, was vulnerable and it was here that the Benedictines concentrated their defences. A fortified harbour, high walls, large defensible towers and a fortified church with machicolations and gun-loops provided substantial defences against opportunistic raiders. This was a substantial monastic establishment founded in the twelfth century. The many agricultural terraces nearby and the construction of a water mill at the entrance of the narrow tidal channel to the inland lake of Veliko Jezero demonstrate the industry of the monks. The nature and typology of the fortifications indicate that the monks maintained and added to the defences over the centuries. Once the headquarters of the Benedictine monks from Dubrovnik, it changed to secular usage in 1869. Derelict by the middle of the twentieth century, its conversion into a hotel and restaurant has altered its appearance, although its strength is still apparent.

## Summary

That so many Christian ecclesiastical fortifications still survive in lands occupied or under the suzerainty of Muslim Ottomans, seems at first sight somewhat paradoxical, especially as they had a policy of destroying secular fortifications not occupied by their army or settlers. That monastic and church defences were not only allowed, but could be kept in a good state of repair is due, not so much to Islamic tolerance, but rather to the Ottoman desire to extract as much tribute as it could from its conquered peoples. Monastic communities were very good at raising tribute in return for their continuing existence. The lawless nature of much of the countryside and coastal regions meant that these producers of wealth needed protection from brigands, warbands and pirates. The Turks realised that it was easier and cheaper for the monks

## Town defences provided by the mendicant orders

Mention has been made of the vast numbers of monasteries built by the mendicant orders either adjacent to city walls or just outside them. Whilst the majority were devoid of fortifications, a number in Italy, as elsewhere, particularly the Holy Roman Empire, lent their bulk to the town defences and acted as bulwarks. Here was a synergy between town and monastery in the mutual defence of their populations. In **Siena** both the Franciscans and the Dominicans built their churches to abut the city walls, that of the former near the east gate and that of the later to protect the western. Both are imposing buildings, although the restoration of the nineteenth century has removed the militaristic façade of the basilica of San Francesco.

Of these monastic bulwarks the finest example, without doubt, is to be found at **Assisi**, the city of St Francis. Viewed from the air two monastic enclosures rise on buttresses from the western aspect of the city. The attached building, to the east, is in fact two churches one built on top of the other, overlying a crypt. The ensemble has something of the air of Albi about it. The upper church, of basilican form with a single nave, protruding transept and single apse, has round towers either side of the apse and semi-circular buttresses at intervals supporting the nave walls. The town of Assisi is built on a hill arising from the plain below Mount Subasio and its mediaeval core is still surrounded by its fortified walls. To the north, at the highest point of the hill, the mediaeval castle of Rocca Maggiore was built for the pope in 1367. Seen from a distance the castle, walls and bulwark of the western complex of churches and monastery appear impregnable.

## Cefalù, Sicily, a fortified cathedral

The gradual return of Sicily to Christianity following its conquest from the Saracens by the Normans during the eleventh and twelfth centuries was marked by the building of magnificent cathedrals incorporating Arab architectural features. Of these imposing buildings the golden sandstone cathedral at **Cefalù** is, perhaps, the finest built by the Normans and their successors, though constructed over two different periods and in two distinct styles. The small fishing port is found on the northern coast of the island and is sheltered by a rocky promontory. It was here that Roger II, the Norman king, started the cathedral in 1133 following a vow that he made when he was in danger of being shipwrecked. First to be built was the apse with its two side chapels, followed by the transept. They are wonderful expressions of power and although there is no active fortification the roofs of the apse and its chapels have stone vaulting, as does the greater part of the transept. To the north of the church was added a cloister for the Augustinian canons who served the church. Although completed by 1148, the nave and western façade was not finished until almost a hundred years later when the Norman rule had been replaced by that of the Hohenstaufen emperors of the Holy Roman Empire. The contrast is dramatic, especially when seen from the side. The nave, dominated by the eastern range, is much less ornate, more austere and decidedly militaristic. The western façade is flanked by two battlemented towers 10m square, similar but slimmer to the powerful minarets of the fortified mosques of Tunisia. Although the openings in the upper storeys are decidedly Romanesque, the merlons of the towers and the side aisles of the nave are Arab in style and are similar to

*Above:* Monastery of St. Simeon, Aswan, Egypt. *Below:* Resafeh, Sergiopolis, Syria

*Above:* Jerpoint Abbey, Co. Kilkenny, Ireland

*Top left:* Glendalough, Ireland

*Middle left:* Kells Priory, Co. Kilkenny, Ireland

*Bottom left:* Rock of Cashel, Co. Tipperary, Ireland

Facing page
*Top:* Crac des Chevaliers, Syria
*Bottom:* Malbork (Marienburg), Poland

*Above left:* Paro dzong, Bhutan. *Above right:* Ta dzong, Trongsa, Bhutan. *Below:* Punakha dzong, Bhutan.

those found on Arab fortifications. The defensive qualities of this striking building are apparent. Although the solitary entrance is sheltered by an open narthex it is covered by arrow loops in the first two storeys of the flanking towers and in the covered gallery running between them. It lends itself to an arch machicolation similar to those at Lincoln. Similar powerful cathedrals were also built at Monreale and Palermo and have a fortified appearance and Arab architectural influences.

Although a secular fortification, the castle of **Ursino** at Catania on the east coast of Sicily bears a striking resemblance in its ground plan to the ribats of North Africa. This castle originally stood on a spit of land jutting out to sea. The eruption of Mount Etna in 1669 enveloped the base of the walls and towers in lava, and the thirteenth-century fabric was not exposed until detailed examination and restoration of the castle was carried out in the 1930s. The original castle, 50m square, was strengthened at the corners by round towers. Semicircular interval towers were added to the middle of all four walls. The internal arrangements are also very similar, with two-storey service rooms with ribbed vaulting aligned against the curtain walls enclosing a small central courtyard. The castle was begun in 1239 by Riccardo da Letini on the orders of Frederick II and was much altered in the fifteenth and sixteenth centuries. Only two corner towers and one interval tower have survived.[5]

There is also evidence that the Arabs built ribats during their conquest and occupation of Sicily and that urban ribats existed in Palermo in the twelfth century.[6]

## Fortified churches and the cortinas of Friuli

Fortified churches are rarely found in either the towns or countryside of Italy probably a result of the changes in the tenth to thirteenth centuries that saw open settlements change to those within fortified walls. As a consequence most churches were built within fortified villages, towns and cities, some becoming part of castle enceintes.

In the north-east of Italy in the region of Friuli, bordering Slovenia, there are a number of peasant defences still surviving, known as cortinas; a few of which contain churches. The north Italian pastoralists constructed their shelters by building platforms of earth, usually 5m high with an average diameter of 100m, and surrounded them with a ditch and vallum on top of which was erected a wooden palisade. Never originally intended for permanent occupation, only three have any remains of buildings.

In many of the hamlets and villages of Europe the church was one of the few buildings worthy of protection and it would seem logical to build the church within the cortina. This is the case at **Carpenteo** near Pozzuolo. Here the earthworks contain the sixteenth-century church of San Michele with its high Gothic windows and in a departure from normal practice the wooden palisade has been replaced by a curtain wall. The tower, which dwarfs the church, guards the solitary entrance reached by a bridge across the ditch. The early peasant defences

---

[5] Anderson (1980: 174) is of the opinion that Islamic influences in the castles built by Frederick in Sicily stemmed from the caravanserai. As the templates for the ribat and the caravanserai are interchangeable this mistake is understandable.

[6] Hillenbrand (2000: 332) quotes the twelfth-century Arab geographer ibn-Hauqal.

attacks in 1571, 1582 and 1611. The fortress monastery became the organising and co-ordinating headquarters for the defence of the whole of the north-west march. Over the sixteenth and seventeenth centuries there developed a symbiotic relationship between the coastal fortresses and settlements overseen by the monastery. Of these the stockaded town of Kem contained a daughter church of the monastery and the citadel of Suma had as its sea-gate a gate-church that acted as a direction beacon for merchant ships. Although built of wood, both fortifications were strong enough to resist Swedish attacks in 1590 and 1591.

The schism in the Church in the middle of the seventeenth century led to the monks of the monastery breaking away from the reformist centralised church, preferring to continue under the old rule. To the monastery and its landholdings flocked many Old Believers, and so successful was the ecclesiastical rebellion that the Tsar despatched an army to besiege and root out the troublemakers. The heroic defence by the monks and their supporters, together with the strength of the fortifications and its island position, enabled them to hold out from 1668 until January 1676, when treachery led to the fall of the monastery and the slaughter of all of its defenders. Returning to the control of Moscow, it became a monastery of the reformed Orthodox Church. It maintained its defences in sufficient order to be able to resist an assault by British warships during the Crimean War.[17]

The blackest period of its history occurred during Stalinist times, when it became one of his infamous concentration camps, where the treatment of prisoners in the punishment cells is described in Solzhenitsyn's book, *The Gulag Archipelago*. It received the attention of the restorers in the 1960s, who returned it to the island monastic fortress of earlier days.

Halfway between Moscow and the White Sea is the Beloye Ozero (White Lake), the source of the River Sheksna, one of the most important trade routes from the forested north to the River Volga. A site of great strategic importance, the monastery of St Cyril at **Belozersk** was founded here over six hundred years ago. Initially remote and inaccessible, it played an important role in the spread of Russian Orthodoxy and in the defence of the northern territories regained by Russia. By the sixteenth century it had become second in size only to the monastery of Zagorsk. Of all the Russian monasteries there are few more imposing sites than the monastic fortifications of St Cyril with its huge buttressed lakeside walls reinforced by enormous square, rectangular and round towers containing tier upon tier of loopholes. The fortifications were originally constructed of wood; the earliest of its stone buildings is the cathedral of the Assumption which dates from 1497. Slowly the wooden defences were replaced by masonry from the first quarter of the sixteenth century. Monastic expansion resulted in the attached, but smaller, monastery of John the Baptist becoming enclosed within defensive walls by the end of the century. Despite being of sufficient strength to resist a prolonged siege by Lithuanians and Poles in 1612–13, the defences subsequently underwent considerable remodelling and rebuilding. The walls seen today date from this period and include the fortifications of the new town erected between 1633 and 1679 to house the lay servants and their families. With three tiers of defensive platforms and a perimeter extending

---

[17] In July 1854, the British warships HMS Eurydice, Brisk and Miranda were looking for an anchorage for a British fleet. There was an exchange of cannon fire and according to monastic history one of the flotilla was sunk. The British version is somewhat different, however.

over 1400m reinforced by thirteen towers it became the finest defensive system of the seventeenth century in Russia's northlands.

# The wooden fortress monasteries of Siberia

The replacement, with brick and stone, of the wooden fortress monasteries of European Russia coincided with the exploration, annexation and colonisation of Siberia, that part of Asia lying to the north of the Islamic khanates of the Golden Horde and reaching to the Arctic seas. The first Russian expedition, a private venture led by Yenuak, had crossed the Urals in 1581.[18] Such was the attraction of the East that in less than a hundred years the Pacific coast had been reached and most of Siberia had been comprehensively surveyed and incorporated into the Russian Empire. It resulted in the mass migrations of Russian peasants in order for the State to exploit the natural resources of this vast wilderness.

To ensure control of these eastern acquisitions by Moscow, the central government over-saw the establishment of fortified custom posts and the tried and tested fortress monasteries. Whereas the continuing wars in the north and west had led to the building of massive fortifications there was no equivalent need in Siberia as the pagan and semi-nomadic tribes, with their primitive weaponry, offered little opposition. The wood-built fortress monasteries were to suffice until they were no longer needed and were then simply allowed to rot away.[19]

Fortunately there are in architectural museums enough remains of these wooden structures to give some idea of their form and construction methods. Archival sources and contemporary illustrations suggest that wooden fortress monasteries closely followed a set typology decreed by Moscow that initially enabled rapid construction of these outpost fortifications. They were built and replaced continuously in Siberia until the middle of the eighteenth century and continued to be so in the Arctic regions until the nineteenth. The last to be built was on the banks of the River Malyy Anyuy, a tributary of the Koloma, in 1840.[20] Usually built at estuaries, along important river trade routes, they proved to be unassailable by the Siberian tribes who did not have firearms.

Examination of the gate-tower, preserved from the monastery of **St Nicholas Korelsky**, erected on the northern bank of the estuary of the River Dvina near Archangel, demonstrates the complexity and culmination of the centuries-long development of wooden monastic fortifications. First mentioned in the archives in the fifteenth century when Russia, isolated from Europe, was trying to establish northern ports to develop a timber trade, it has been rebuilt many times. Unlike many of the wooden buildings of Siberia from the late Middle Ages it has managed to survive. Restoration towards the end of the nineteenth century enabled the fortifications to survive, at least in part, until the gate-tower was transferred to the open-air

---

[18] It was the conquest of the khanate of Kazan, in 1552, which allowed the Russians to penetrate Siberia and exploit the lucrative fur trade of the region. The discovery of mineral deposits, especially copper and silver and rich fisheries contributed to its rapid colonisation.

[19] Hamilton (1983: 165) points out that although many churches have been preserved from the seventeenth and eighteenth centuries, their fortifications have been allowed to rot away.

[20] Opolovnikov and Opolovnikov (1989: 86).

to live under the supervision of the Franciscans. The garrison of the undefended presidio varied from decade to decade but was never big enough to provide the security the missions needed if they were to prosper. The destruction of the Texan mission of Santa Cruz de San Saba, built to try to pacify some of the Apache groups, and the massacre of many of its inhabitants by the Commanches and their allies in 1758 provided the stimulus for the friars to fortify the Alamo. The plaza of the mission, to the west of the church and convento was enclosed with an adobe and stone wall almost 3m high and 1m thick with primitive bastions for the small artillery pieces supplied by the military. Measuring approximately 145m (north to south) by 50m (east to west), this irregular rectangular enclosure contained the lodgings for the natives. The solitary gateway located in the southern stretch is recorded as being defended by a tower and three canons in 1762. Ordered to be secularised in 1793 the mission lost its religious, pastural and educative role and became an army post for a squadron of Spanish regular cavalry sent to protect San Antonio. It had become in fact the de facto presidio. Such was the instability of the region that between 1810 and 1865 the former mission had sixteen different occupiers. Alterations from this period and the subsequent encroachment of the town have resulted in the destruction of much of the mission buildings of the eighteenth century. What remain have been carefully restored.

Also on the banks of the San Antonio River, but several kilometres to the south of the Alamo, is the mission of **San José y San Miguel de Aguayo**. Relocated in 1739 after an epidemic had decimated the mission population the stone-built friary extends eastwards from the church and contained a granary and workshops for weavers, blacksmiths and carpenters. Towards the end of its life as a mission one of the friars, Fray José Pedrago, had built a flour mill powered by water. Possessing a large tract of land along the river the irrigation scheme, or acequia, of the mission ensured abundant crops of corn, potatoes, beans, sugar cane and cotton, whilst the ranch held thousands of cattle, sheep and goats. Its riches proved tempting to the Apaches and by 1768 the mission had become enclosed by a defensive wall to protect its three hundred or so inhabitants. Each wall had a gateway and towers overlooked the walls and gates. When visited by Morfi in 1777 the mission was described as being strongly fortified and the first mission in America.[32]

The remaining three missions in San Antonio, **San Juan**, **Concepción** and **Espada** were similarly fortified and defended by their occupants and small detachments of presidio troops. In response to Apache incursions these had increased to eighty by 1772, twenty of whom were stationed outside the town to protect rancher settlers and travellers to La Bahia to the south-east. All the missions were to become secularised by the turn of the nineteenth century and property and land given to the mission inhabitants. As in Mexico this had been the intention from the outset.

Kennedy has attempted to compare these fortified churches and missions of Spanish New Mexico and Texas with the ribats of North Africa.[33] He is undoubtedly correct in his belief that

[32] Juan Agustín Morfi was a Spanish Franciscan missionary and historian who accompanied Teodoro de Croix, the newly appointed commandant general of the provinces on his inspection tour. He compiled an early history of Texas.
[33] Kennedy (1993: 68–70).

Moorish architectural influences were transported across the Atlantic to the Americas. His claims, however, that the ruins of the fortified missions along the frontiers of New Spain are indistinguishable from the ribat ruins of North Africa do not hold up when typology and occupancy are compared. It is only in the context that both provided frontier defences along the frontier against hostile enemies that any comparison is achieved. A more plausible influence may have been the large Friday mosques of Islam, which like the fortress monasteries of Mexico with their atrio could accommodate thousands of worshippers. Both the mosque courtyard and mission atrio are surrounded by walls, fortified in many instances, and arcaded to provide protection from the sun. Certainly the friar architects would have been familiar with the great Moorish mosques of the Iberian peninsula.

# The eighteenth-century missions and presidios of California

Although the missions of California were not themselves fortified four were protected by the neighbouring presidios of San Diego de Alcalá (1769), Monterey (1770), San Francisco (1776) and Santa Barbara (1782) continuing the tradition established earlier on the Spanish–American frontier of using mission and presidio to establish colonial settlements.

By 1823, twenty-one missions had been established along the Californian littoral, each a good day's walk from the next and joined by El Camino Real or the Royal Road. The need for protection by presidios was not from any threat from the Californian native tribes but rather the fear of English privateers and Russian advances down the eastern seaboard.[34] Although the Franciscan missionaries recruited from Spain wished to maintain segregated mission communities, the influx of Hispanic settlers resulted in the opening up of the missions to Spanish residents. By 1846 all had become secularised.

# The missions amongst the Maya of the Yucatan peninsula

The Yucatan peninsula in the south-east of Mexico juts out from the mainland into the Gulf of Mexico to the north-west and the Caribbean to the east. Densely populated by the Maya when accidentally discovered by the Spanish in 1511, it proved to be one of the most difficult regions to subdue, control and colonise.[35] The Spanish entradas of the first half of the sixteenth century met fierce resistance from the Mayan tribes until a combination of famine and a smallpox epidemic eroded their resolve and enabled the Spaniards to occupy the whole of the peninsula by 1545. The attempted spiritual conquest began shortly afterwards when eight Franciscan friars were invited into Yucatan.

The first mission to be founded was at Campeche, a coastal Spanish settlement, soon to be followed by the main Franciscan mission in the newly established capital of Mérida in the

[34]  Ibid. 19. Kennedy describes the indigenous population of California as comprising of docile urban societies similar to the Mexican and Guaraní natives. If any threat had existed the huge mortality from diseases introduced from Europe rendered the natives powerless.

[35]  Ruled from Spain and not Mexico City until Mexican independence, the peninsula was originally believed to be an island. It is essentially an immense limestone plateau with few natural resources and poor agricultural land.

Christian despite repeated incursions and invasions by its Muslim neighbours. The cycle of destruction and renaissance is ingrained in Georgian culture, and the erection of churches, often on the top of mountains, is a visible expression of defiance and an unconquerable will.

Georgia fought a strenuous war against the Arab invaders of the seventh century, enabling monasticism not only to survive but also to flourish so that by the tenth century it been able to extended its influence beyond the country's borders to Greece and Palestine. It coincided with the finest period of ecclesiastical building, culminating in the construction of the magnificent cathedrals of Sveti-Cxoveli, Alaverdi and the church of Bagrat at Kutaisi.

Although the mountainous nature of the country together with the emergence of rulers determined to obtain and maintain independence from their Muslim neighbours has enabled Georgia to flourish, the thirteenth century heralded a progressive erosion of Georgian nationality, finally sealed by the capture of Constantinople. Georgia became subject to repeated invasions by both Turks and Persians. National unity was replaced with warring dukedoms or Muslim suzerainty. The only building works of any significance were fortifications. Architecture became impoverished and subject to Persian influences, seen in the use of brick. The isolated and elevated positions of many churches and monasteries were natural sites easily defended, and most of Georgia's rural ecclesiastical buildings were fortified to some extent. They were kept in good repair until Russia was invited to come to the country's aid in the nineteenth century.

## The fortified monastic cave-city of Vardzia

The River Kura, arising in Turkey, winds its way through the mountains that straddle north-eastern Turkey and south-west Georgia. This high mountain valley became a natural invasion route. Cave-dwellings and rock-cut monasteries were already established in the area when King Giorgi III (1156–84) turned his attention to the tenth-century cave-village of **Vardzia** in an attempt to bar an invasion route and defend his country from the Turks. To the cave-village he added a fortified cave-monastery, excavated out of the tufaceous rock of the mountainside.

At first sight, the monastery added to the earlier secular habitations looks indefensible and yet it became a repository for national treasures and a refuge for the civil population for over three centuries. The appearance today, however, differs markedly from how it looked originally. Damage to the cliff face, both natural and man-made, has exposed many of the cave galleries, tunnels and staircases that connected them and were originally hidden from view.

Rising to a height of 3300m above sea level, the mountain face was cut away to steepen its river frontage. Into the soft tuffa were excavated hundreds of caves and galleries, hollowed out in a north–south direction, often reaching 50m in depth. It also became a multi-tiered complex of between seven and thirteen storeys extending along a frontage running east to west and measuring over 500m. Today, an external thirteenth-century bell-tower demarcates the division between the earlier cave-dwellings and the contemporary cave-monastery. However, the civil settlement was gradually absorbed into the monastery over the centuries and any distinction lost.

There are no external fortifications visible today, but the steep cliff face makes access to the cave entrances almost impossible other than at the lowest western end where the monastic stables lay. A complex system of guard chambers, narrow tunnels between individual rooms and vertical shafts between each tier of caves controlled egress and ingress. Subterranean galleries with tunnels to the outside were camouflaged so that their role in providing rallying points for a rapid sortie outside the complex were completely hidden.

Archaeologists have so far discovered over five hundred rooms serving as churches and monastic buildings. Water was obtained from a natural spring in the heart of the mountain and by a subterranean aqueduct with a complex distribution system. Two churches are outstanding; both the central church of the Assumption, damaged in the earthquake of 1283, and the church of the Transfiguration are decorated with magnificent frescoes painted between the twelfth and sixteenth centuries.[7]

For centuries the monastery was a Christian frontier fortification of strength and served its purpose well against both Turks and Persians until Persian forces, led by Shah Tahmasp, captured the cave complex in 1551. Its appearance today, despite the damage that has changed it externally, is one of great strength. Although only a fraction of the rooms and tunnels are open to visitors, the complexity and defensibility of this cave monastery is apparent. It fell only when the Georgian army of King Luarsab I of Kartli was defeated by that of Shah Tahmasp and resistance would serve no purpose.

### The fortified churches of Dzhvari, Ninocminda and Ananuri

Overlooking the monastic fortress town of Mcxeta, at the confluence of the Aragivi and Kura Rivers 18km north of Tbilisi, is the fortified church of **Dzhvari**. It is a fine example of the Georgian propensity for choosing hill-top sites that dominate the countryside; the church is visible from all around. As is common in Georgian ecclesiastical fortifications, the church and its defences are from two separate eras, in this instance a thousand years apart, the first being from 586 to 605. Entirely Georgian in design and concept, it was one of a number built throughout Georgia in the sixth and seventh centuries, at a time when the country had still to be united politically.[8] The exceptionally fine ashlar construction together with its complementary sculpture contrasts markedly with the poor quality of its surrounding stone and brick fortifications, obviously hastily built to protect one of the national symbols of Georgia. The site lends itself to defence falling away steeply down to the river hundreds of metres below. Here the western apse of the church is incorporated into the curtain wall. The more gently sloping south and eastern approaches are strongly fortified with high walls and multi-storey towers used for the accommodation of the defenders. The north-eastern tower is the strongest. The solitary entrance, in the south-east, is further protected by a barbican, now much ruined. Built of field stone with brick and tiles framing loopholes and openings in the towers, it was a substantial castle church. That it was meant as a serious defensive outpost, overlooking the monastic town below, is shown by the construction of a substantial cistern

---

[7] Cave complexes and huge underground cities were used by the Christians of Cappadocia in Asia Minor for centuries and achieved a high degree of sophistication.

[8] Beridze et al. (1984: 38). The church is described as being a tetraconch, whereby four apses point in the cardinal directions of the compass. Although regarded as being entirely Georgian, there was a separate and parallel development in Armenia.

the basilican plan. Three other forms now appeared. Pankhurst reproduces the eyewitness account of Father Paes who had travelled extensively in Ethiopia; he observed that in addition to the basilican churches some were round, some square and some rectangular. He also mentioned that some seemed to him 'to resemble a fortress in their massive character'.[19]

In general terms the rectangular church is an earlier development than the round and is more common in the north of Ethiopia, whereas overall there are more round churches. Examples of both rectangular and round churches with attendant fortifications are found in the highlands but the numbers cannot even be guessed at. Of those round churches visited all are enclosed within at least one substantial oval or circular wall built of dry stone or field-stone in a mud mortar; the entrance is a gateway, often of two storeys. Its function is almost certainly defensive, probably, however, to protect the graves from the attentions of wild animals.

## Impressions

Ethiopia contains thousands of churches that have yet to be studied. Despite long periods of warfare and civil unrest many churches contain wall paintings, illuminated manuscripts and records seen by few. Many date from centuries ago. There are, however, enough churches that remain fortified and are accessible to suggest that there may be many more churches and monasteries that received similar fortifications even if only against wild animals and Shifta brigands, especially in rural areas.

Such has been the suffering of this magnificent country and its peoples for hundreds of years that it faces many important tasks and lacks the resources required to survey the vast numbers of churches and monasteries. A flight over the Highlands reveals large numbers of isolated and walled round churches. Jager, Pearce and Plant have shown what can be achieved by persistent fieldwork. The latter has demonstrated that there are archives, so far inaccessible, kept by church authorities in the provincial townships. It is impossible, however, to know the damage done during the civil wars of recent times and the extent of the loss of such archives.

---

[19] Pankhurst (1955: 340).

# 14
# ISLAM I

## Introduction

Byzantium had long perceived that the greatest threat to its Middle Eastern and Egyptian provinces came from the Sassanian Empire, which coveted the riches of Syria, Asia Minor and Egypt. So concerned with each other were these two great empires that they totally neglected, and failed to recognise, what was happening in the Arabian peninsula.

By the time of his death in 632, Muhammad had succeeded in unifying nearly all the tribes of Arabia, spiritually and politically, into the embryonic Islamic nation, soon to unleash its enormous, but as yet dormant, military might on a world exhausted by almost continuous conflict.

The success of the Arab army in Palestine, at the Battle of Ajnadyn in 634, over a punitive Byzantine expeditionary force, led to a series of brilliant military campaigns; armies spread out from Arabia: westwards into North Africa: eastwards into central Asia. Expansion was rapid; Tripoli had been reached in 644, although it was to be a further one hundred years before the rest of North Africa and Spain became part of the Islamic Empire. Kabul, in Afghanistan, fell in 664, opening the way to India. To the north, a contracted Byzantine Empire continued to hold out. In just over a hundred years the Islamic Empire stretched from northern India in the east to southern France in the west.

The failure to take Constantinople in the eighth century saw a change of tack; Muslim rulers opted for consolidation rather than expansion.[1] Temporary camps for a rapidly advancing army needed to be replaced by more permanent fortifications for occupying garrisons, especially on the borders; lines of communication had to be secured and the Arab minority protected.

## The influences of early Roman and Byzantine fortifications

As Cresswell points out, fortifications were all but unknown in Arabia before the Islamic conquests.[2] The early invading armies, who had travelled north into Syria, came into contact with the Roman Byzantine frontier forts which ran in a chain from the Gulf of Aqaba to Palmyra, north-east of Damascus. Known as the castra of the Roman Limes Arabicus, originally built at the time of Trajan and Diocletian, they had been maintained and garrisoned for centuries. The basic plan had been replicated throughout the Roman Empire; those inherited by the Byzantine Empire underwent major renovations and additions, especially during the

---

[1]  Hillenbrand (1999: 93).
[2]  Cresswell (1952: 89–91). This is still the best paper on the subject of Arab fortifications before 1250. It does, however, need updating in the light of new studies.

reign of Justinian in the sixth century. These forts were square or rectangular, with square or round corner towers and half-round or square interval towers, designed to accommodate the artillery of the period, surrounding a central courtyard. There was a solitary entrance, frequently defended by a portcullis and often integral with an interval tower. Internally they contained barracks, officers' quarters and rooms for the quartermaster's stores and equipment. Great attention was paid to cisterns for the storage of water and in the provision of wells, especially in arid regions.

It is from the early military architects of these enduring forts, particularly those of Justinian, that later generations of military engineers, both Islamic and Christian, took so many ideas in their development of the fort and the castle.

Cresswell argues that some of the frontier forts in Syria were first used by the Umayyad princes, and their soldiery, who gleaned the necessary knowledge to enable the Arabs to construct their own fortifications, using the huge pool of skilled builders available to the conquerors. He cites the **Qasr al-Hair West**, built by Caliph Hisham in 727, on the road from Damascus to Palmyra, as the first of the purely Islamic fortifications to be built. Hisham had chosen to build what is considered a fortified palace on a small knoll in the Syrian steppe, incorporating the tall watchtower of the Justinian monastery, previously occupying the site. This is of importance as it contained an earlier machicolation, a defensive projection, overlooking and protecting the only entrance to the monastery. It is considered to be the forerunner of a form of military architecture soon to become commonplace in Islamic fortifications but not to reach Europe until the twelfth century.[3] The contemporary fortified palace of **Qasr al-Hair East** comprises two adjacent buildings; it represents a stage in the development of Umayyad military architecture, incorporating, as it does, machicolations. Greatly influenced by the architecture of the earlier frontier forts, they follow a similar ground plan and became the basic template for the future development of Islamic architecture, encompassing, with necessary modifications relative to function, the ribat, mosque, caravanserai, khan, madrasa and khanaqah.[4]

The eastern borders of this new Arab Empire, before further expansion into Asia and India, coincided with those of the Persian Sassanian Empire, and little in the way of new fortification was needed; existing defences were adequate. This was not the position on its borders with the Byzantine Empire; the Syrian, Palestinian, Egyptian and North African provinces had been lost but the Greek Byzantine core was far from moribund. It still posed a considerable threat to Islamic territories, especially to Syria and, via its naval strength, to North Africa, which was also threatened by the Berbers, nomadic camel-herding pasturalists from its neighbouring inland, mountain and desert regions.

The caliphs countered the threat, in part, in a uniquely Islamic way; architectural, secular,

---

[3] The palace gateway had a façade, decorated in carved stucco, believed to be the earliest example in Islamic architecture; fortunately still preserved in the National Museum in Damascus.

[4] Hillenbrand (1994: 334) points out that Islamic architecture uses the same form for different functions. He is of the opinion that the palace forts of Cresswell may well have served as caravanserai (q.v.), and that the influence of the Roman castrum was unlikely to have spread beyond Roman territory in the Near East.

# The RIBATS of Islam
## Fortress Monasteries of the borderlands

The ground plans of the Ribats of
SOUSSE and MONASTIR
compared with those of
DAYAKHATYN, KHARANA
& Qasr Al~HAIR ASH~SHARQI

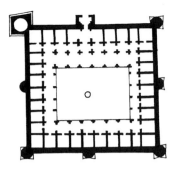

SOUSSE
Tunisian RIBATS
MONASTIR

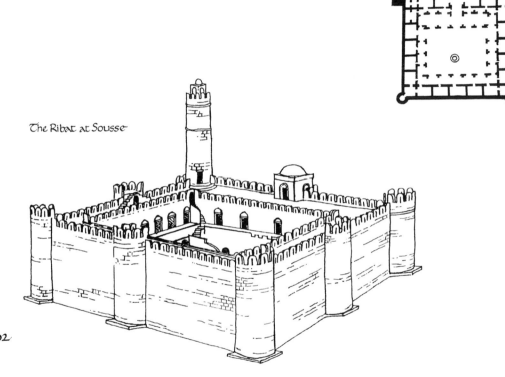

The Ribat at Sousse

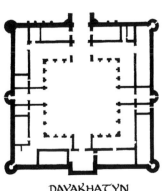

DAYAKHATYN
11th century caravanserai
Uzbekistan

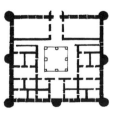

Scales are approximate

Qasr KHARANA
fortified palace c. 710
Jordan

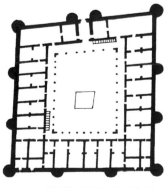

Qasr Al~HAIR ASH~SHARQI east
727 Caliphal residence 729
Syria

military, religious and conceptual considerations were brought together to produce the ribat.

It is difficult to define what, at first glance, appears to be a distinct morphological fortification, with its uniquely Islamic garrison, the Murabitun ('men of the ribat'), a confraternity of the 'Guardians of Islam'. Our knowledge of the role and function of the ribat is derived, to a large degree, from literary sources, although recent excavations in Tunisia and Spain, together with the work of Neji Djelloul is altering Western concepts of this specialised fortification. Built in their thousands throughout the Islamic Empire, over a period spanning four centuries, especially on the borders with Byzantium, in Central Asia, North Africa and in the Iberian peninsula, surviving examples are few. With one exception (the ribat of Guardamar del Segura, in Spain), all are to be found on the coast of the Maghreb[5], especially Tunisia; dating just before and during the Aghlabid dynasty (800–909); a time of great prosperity and territorial ambitions.

Carole Hillenbrand proffers a simple definition. Writing about Arab fortifications at the time of the Crusades she defines the ribat as a 'frontier fort in which jihad fighters lived according to strict religio-military rule'.[6] Djelloul widens the definition substantially, after studying the fortifications in Tunisia, especially of Sousse and Monastir, following recent archaeological discoveries. Whilst happily accepting that ribats existed in isolation from other fortifications and buildings, he postulates that ribats were also part of a conglomeration of buildings, serving at times to house vast numbers of Murabitun and to be integral parts of town fortifications. He does not believe that the term ribat should be confined to a specific building type, suggesting that these conglomerations were, in effect, 'une ville-ribat' specifically to accommodate the ascetic warrior monks.[7] This theory will be explored further when the fortifications of Sousse and Monastir come to be examined in detail.

Ribats have been likened in the West to fortress monasteries and their garrisons compared to the warrior monks of the later Christian military orders. Whilst there are undoubted similarities there are also fundamental differences. Before the typology and role of the ribat are considered, it is necessary to understand the nature of jihad and the part played by the Murabitun.

## Jihad, the 'path of God' and the role of the Murabitun, the 'soldiers of the Faith'

Ribats can be considered to be successors to the Roman castra and the Byzantine frontier forts. They came into being around the eighth century when the frontiers of the Islamic world became stabilised and secure lines of communication were needed. Placed on the borders of lands threatening Islam and the less secure regions of newly conquered territories, they needed tough, disciplined and committed garrisons. The formal concept of jihad, or Holy War, waged by the followers of the Prophet Muhammad against the infidel had by this

[5]   That part of North Africa now comprising the countries of Libya, Tunisia, Algeria and Morocco.
[6]   Hillenbrand (1999: 100–1).
[7]   Djelloul (1999: 42–53).

time become inculcated by the Qur'an and tradition into the Islamic consciousness; the Murabitun were ideally placed to promote this notion. The first in the class of warrior monks, they predate their Western counterparts by four centuries. Although military skills and pious asceticism were very similar, there was one fundamental difference; unlike in the Christian orders, a Murabit served the cause of Allah for an agreed and variable period of time; unlike the Christian monastic orders, Islam has no concept of permanent vows.[8] Elena Lourie points out that this notion of 'stints of service' is the most striking feature of the ribat. Service as a Murabit in the ribat was a voluntary act of piety for a variable and agreed period. Recruitment was never a problem as membership of this brotherhood conferred considerable benefits both secular and religious upon the volunteer; calling upon others to join the Murabitun was especially meritous and ensured a constant supply of volunteers. The opportunity for a pious and ascetic life, together with the very real chance of martyrdom, ensured the commitment of these Arab holy warriors to jihad.[9] As a member of the jund, the ruling Arab elite, albeit with a duty of care to the neighbouring indigenous population whether Muslim or not, service in a ribat was accepted as a worthy substitute for prayer and fasting. It also ensured that the warrior monk would also gain entry into paradise, whether martyred during jihad or not.

The initial role of the Murabitun was to take the leading part in the defence of the borders of Islam and, on occasions, be part of expeditionary forces seeking to enlarge the world of Islam. Jihad could therefore be both passively and actively engaged in. At the beginning, there was no missionary role, but this changed when the indigenous population started to convert to Islam. When Arabic was adopted as the universal language of the lands of Islam and non-Arabs became assimilated, proselytising became increasingly important and with the inroads made by the heretical Shiites, the Murabitun increasingly preached the Faith, seeking conversions to the orthodox Sunni sect of Islam.

Djelloul has widened the definition of the ribat, at the same time arguing that the Murabitun took on additional duties. Those serving in coastal ribats and ville-ribats acted as coastguards warning and protecting the civil population against raids by the Byzantine navy where possible. They also accepted responsibility for the care of refugees and victims of such raids, finally involving themselves in the negotiations for the ransom and release of Islamic prisoners. They became military instructors, training a citizen militia to defend the walled cities springing up in the wake of conquest, frequently in the vicinity of their ribat. They also played an important role in the training of volunteers for jihad.[10]

Despite the widening role of the Murabit, he remained primarily a warrior monk. Asceticism and Islam were central to his main purpose of defending the Dar al-Islam, the 'Abode of Peace', against the infidel, whether by passively defending its borders or by actively pursuing an offensive jihad into the Dar al-Harb, the 'Abode of War'.

---

[8]  Lourie (1982: 167–8, 170). She also argues that, even if temporary service was borrowed from the Murabit, it could never be applied to warrior monks, only to lay brothers, citing the attachment, to the Order of the Temple, of knights who served for a short period only.

[9]  Lapidus (1991: 368).

[10]  Djelloul (1999: 44–6).

a legacy to its mediaeval past. Although now surrounded by restaurants and souvenir shops, careful and sympathetic restoration gives us a rare insight into the morphology of a ribat; only the parapet with its crenellations are modern and these are based on similar structures from the Aghlabid period.

The accretions of centuries have been removed to expose the ribat; architectural features developed in Syria during the Aghlabid period are instantly recognisable. From the outside the light brown sandstone blocks, carefully coursed, impart a warmth today that belies its militant and ascetic past. Enclosed within the town walls of 859, the ribat, constructed on top of the ruins of a sixth-century Byzantine fort, is a two-storey crenellated building, approximately 38m square. Strengthened by round corner towers except at the south-eastern angle where the corner tower is square and solid to wall height. It supports a cylindrical tower surmounted by a cupola. Access is reached from the wall walk by a spiral staircase. Known as the Nador tower, dating from 821, it served as a lookout tower, signalling beacon and possibly as a minaret. In the middle of the north, east and west curtain walls solid semi-circular buttress towers rise a little above the battlemented enceinte. The solitary entrance is by way of a square interval tower in the middle of the southern wall.

Built of regular courses of rough-hewn ashlar sandstone blocks, no consideration was given to decoration with the exception of the archway of the southern gateway.[13] Here, classical marble columns from the Roman epoch, that on the left fluted, stand on square podiums. The finely carved capitals and partial lintel above (also delicately carved and from antiquity) are surmounted by voussoirs so arranged as to be instantly recognisable as a very early version of the colloquially known Moorish or 'horseshoe' shaped archway. This fine portal leads to the purely military entrance passage; barrel-vaulted, with guard-rooms arranged on either side, additional defence is provided by a portcullis and two arch machicolations to enable defenders to rain down missiles on an enemy attempting to breach the gateway and held up by the portcullis. Further obstruction is provided by a double-planked, iron-sheathed and studded door.

The enceinte surrounds a central courtyard containing a well. Against the four walls at ground-floor level are arranged rooms, reputedly for military supplies and stores. Examination of a number of rooms reveals (as is confirmed in a number of ribats where the ground-floor arrangements exist, especially in Monastir) some of these rooms provided with stone benches and water channels, suggesting that the kitchen, refectory and stables were also on the ground floor. An arched cloister runs around the outside of these rooms and provides the walkway for the first-storey cells for the Murabitun, which are placed against all but the southern wall. Access to these cells, the walkway and the Nador tower is by means of staircases from both the south-eastern and south-western corners of the courtyard. Against the southern wall, above the gateway and the guard-rooms, the prayer hall of the mosque runs the whole length. Interestingly, it is pierced for the movable missile-firing artillery of the early Middle Ages. The loopholed crenellations that run round the external wall of the fort also run round the internal edge of the walkway so that defence was sustainable even if the courtyard was penetrated.

The spartan, simple lifestyle of these 'Defenders of the Faith', is echoed everywhere in this

---

[13] The blind arcading running all round the parapet under the string course of the loopholed crenellations of the southern wall and towers is part of the modern restoration.

building; whilst it would be able to accommodate a significant population, if necessary, the twenty or so cells would indicate a comparatively small resident garrison.

The ribat at Sousse is a near neighbour to the contemporary fortified mosque and the town walls near to the harbour. Djelloul is of the opinion that it is the sole remaining ribat of the ville-ribat of Sousse, the most important naval base in Ifriqya during the Aghlabid period, and cites other ribats that existed in Sousse and nearby al-Kantawi.[14] There are no remains of any of these associated ribats today; this is not the case at Monastir, however.

## The ville-ribat of Monastir, one of the 'Gates of Paradise'

Situated on the coast, less than 25km south of Sousse, the ribat of **Monastir**, now part of the kasbah, was built in 796 by the Abbasid governor Harthama ibn-Ayun. Much altered, the ribat underwent considerable change in the eleventh century, when it became enveloped in a much larger enceinte. Reinforced with square flanking towers, it became the citadel of the walled town and received many additions to its fortifications over the ensuing centuries, culminating in the eighteenth-century artillery bastion at its north-eastern corner, which overlooked the harbour.

Approximately one third of the eighth-century ribat still remains; fortunately the southern wall remains in its entirety, replicating, faithfully, the Nador tower, southern gateway and the prayer hall of the ribat of Sousse. Archaeological evidence supports the view that, although somewhat smaller (33m square), it exhibited, in almost every detail, the same architectural features. Like Sousse, it lies close to the Friday mosque. The decision in the early part of the 1960s to demolish much of the medina of Monastir, especially that part around the kasbah, revealed the ground plans of two nearby ribats dating from the same Aghlabid period. Archaeological excavations on the small islet of Sidi al-Ghadamisi overlooking the harbour has revealed the foundations of a further ribat. All conform in almost every detail to the ground plan of the ribat of Sousse. It is this grouping of mainland ribats, surrounded by a fortified enceinte, enclosing the Friday mosque, barracks and lodgings specifically for Murabitun that Djelloul has called the ville-ribat, a township designed to accommodate only the warrior monks.

## The ribats and ville-ribats of the Ifriqyan coast

The Aghlabid period coincided not only with a period of great prosperity, but also with a period of increased military activity in the Eastern Mediterranean. Jihad had been proclaimed by the Aghlabids as a means to further their designs on Sardinia, Sicily, southern Italy and Malta. The Byzantines responded by sending their still powerful fleet to harry the North African coast and disrupt the preparations of the Murabitun and the levies of the Aghlabids. As a consequence, the embarkation ports and harbours received their villes-ribats, from Gabes in the south to Bizerte in the north, connected by a chain of individual ribats all round the coastline. From the evidence of the recently discovered ribat of **Lamta**, 12km south-east of

[14] Djelloul (1999: 42).

are deeply grooved after centuries of friction from the ropes used to haul up water in leather buckets from these internal reservoirs.

The three-storey minaret is incorporated into the northern wall in line with the mihrab. Although the lower courses of the first storey date from around 725, the rest of this minaret dates from the ninth century. This is undoubtedly a military tower.

Kairouan was the first city founded by the Arabs in North Africa, around 670, and had its origins in the military camp of the occupying army. The appearance of the ninth-century mosque, the most important Islamic building in Africa, together with its crenellated minaret supports Djelloul's assertion that it is a 'fort constituting a symbol for the community and its prayers'.[4]

The surrounding city walls, reinforced with round towers and fortified gateways, were first built in the twelfth century. Thus for almost three hundred years the Great Mosque served as a fortified citadel for the invading Arabs and as with Christian and Buddhist monumental fortified buildings was symbolic of the power and permanence of the religion.

The mosques at Tunis and Sfax, both in Tunisia, date from the ninth century and follow Kairouan very closely in ground plan and minaret, displaying the same military countenance, although there is a departure in form at the mosque at Sousse, already mentioned in connection with its neighbouring ribat. Buttresses are absent and the much smaller mosque has no minaret, defence being provided by substantial corner towers and a battlemented parapet.

## The mosque as part of urban fortifications

Four surviving examples have been identified where the walls of the mosque have become an integral part of the defences of a city, analogous to the incorporation of Christian churches and cathedrals into the fortified enceintes of cities. Each needs to be examined separately, belonging as they do to different periods and different dynasties.

Mahdia, founded in 916 on the Tunisian coast, shortly after the arrival of the first of the Fatimid caliphs, became their capital in 921. Planned from the outset to serve a number of roles, the site was chosen because of its strategic position and ease of defence. A spit of land that jutted out from the eastern Sahel coast of Ifriqya separated by a narrow sandy isthmus from the mainland was chosen. A triple layer of walls defended the landward side and the rest of the spit was surrounded by seawalls. Designed from the start as a royal city for the caliph and his court (commoners and merchants were housed in a suburb on the landward side), it contained the port, probably previously excavated by the Phoenicians, and the arsenal for the emerging Fatimid navy. Cisterns, reservoirs and storage buildings, so necessary in times of siege, were installed, along with fortified palaces for the nobility. The mosque, the first built by the Fatimids, was an integral part of the seaward defences on the south and occupied reclaimed land where the western and southern walls formed part of the ramparts of the city. Curiously, the two corner towers of the façade of the mosque contain water tanks. Unfortunately the present mosque is recent; it was rebuilt between 1961 and 1965, faithfully reproducing the tenth-century plan that still exists.

[4] Djelloul (2000: 8).

Mahdia successfully resisted sieges in 945, 1390 and again in 1520 by the Spaniards, only to fall in 1555 during the Habsburg–Ottoman conflict, when most of the defences, including those provided by the mosque, were destroyed.

Two mosques in Cairo occupy part of the stone walls built by the Fatimid vizier Badr al-Jamali between 1087 and 1092, so enlarging the fortified city and replacing an earlier mud-brick wall. The mosque of al-Hakim, built between 990 and 1013, is a square enclosure mosque measuring 120 x 115m, constructed in brick with its outer walls faced with roughly dressed stone. Originally outside the defences of the city, the north-eastern wall of the mosque became incorporated in the city wall between the Bab al-Futuh (the gate of prosperity) and the Bab al-Nasr (the gate of glory). The two minarets, originally separated from the mosque became embedded in square bastions; that at the northern angle becoming one of the battlemented towers of the city wall. This mosque, the second to be built by the Fatimids, has many similarities with the mosque in Mahdia. It suffered in the earthquake of 1302 and has undergone a number of renovations and changes of use. When housing prisoners of war during the Crusades, the Franks built inside a chapel, destroyed when Saladin turned the mosque into stabling for his cavalry. During the French occupation of Egypt by Napoleon it became a fortress and storehouse for the invading army, finally becoming, in the nineteenth century, a repository for many of the precious artefacts of Islam. More recently it has returned to its original role and serves as a mosque for the Ismaili Shiite sect.

The mosque of Mu'ayyad Shaykh, a Circassian slave who rose to become an emir in the fifteenth century, abuts the Bab Zuwaylah, a gateway built in the southern wall around 1092. It is debatable whether this mosque was truly fortified; however, its southern wall is contiguous with the city wall and the solidity of the flanking drum towers of the attached city gate was used to support the two elegant, slim and octagonal minarets built in 1419 and 1420.

The walls of **Jerusalem** have undergone much rebuilding and represent work of many periods, Byzantine, Umayyad, Crusader, Mamluk and Ottoman; the walls remaining today are the work of Suleyman II who rebuilt the walls of Jerusalem which incorporated the Haram esh-Sharif, the 'Noble Sanctuary of Islam'. Known also as the Temple Mount, it is no less holy to the Jews, whose Temple stood here, and to Christians as a consequence of the role it played in the life of Jesus. It is here that the Rock of Abraham, protected by the Dome of the Rock, is found, together with the Aqsa mosque, the end point of Muhammad's miraculous night journey from the holy mosque of Mecca. The Haram esh-Sharif is the third most holy site of Islam and the Aqsa mosque occupies much of the south side and abuts the southern outer wall of the Temple and the double gate of the city fortifications. Founded during the Umayyad period and contemporary with the great mosque of Damascus, its present form dates from the middle of the fourteenth century.

# The minaret, its origins and function

Instantly recognisable, the origin and early function of the minaret is the subject of much discussion, most of it speculative. It is a widely held view that it is a tall slim tower, closely associated with a mosque, whence the Muezzin calls the faithful to the Adhan, the ritual prayers of Islam performed five times daily.

Minarets fall into two main categories: the tall, round and slim towers of the eastern lands of Islam, and the large square towers of North Africa, found occasionally also in Spain.[5] Whilst the former probably owe their origin to the lookout and beacon towers of the Middle Eastern and Asian caravan routes and possibly the Syrian church bell-tower it is claimed that the **Pharos** lighthouse in Alexandria provided the role model for the military-looking minarets of Ifriqya. Regarded as one of the wonders of the world, the Pharos was built in antiquity and was the centre of a line of lighthouses stretching along the coast both eastwards and westwards. Reputably over 100m tall this three-storey tapering building held in its top storey a lighting apparatus visible for 50km. It continued to function long after the Arab conquest of 641 but the lighting apparatus was replaced by a mosque after the earthquake damage of 1100 until finally being destroyed by another earthquake a couple of centuries later.

The minaret at **Kairouan** is much smaller, however, although also of three storeys. Measuring 10.5m square at its base, it rises to a height of 31.5m. The lower storey is thick-walled and loopholed on three of its four faces. The side overlooking the open courtyard of the mosque contains the solitary entrance doorway with its intricately carved lintel and small windows, one for each of the three floors. From its loopholed battlements rises the second storey, smaller to allow for a wall walk for the defenders, and provided with battlements and surmounted by a third storey, a ribbed cupola. It is now believed that this military-looking tower was based on the Roman lighthouse of Salakta, on the nearby coast, itself modelled on the Pharos.

Support for the belief that the main function of the Kairouan minaret was as a defence tower is provided by the appearance of the Khalaf tower in the kasbah of the coastal town of Sousse, east of Kairouan. This battlemented tower, 8m square at its base, rises to a height of 30m. The four floors are reached by a staircase built into the thickness of the walls, and the first served as a mosque for the watchmen. Built on the highest point in the city, it served as a lighthouse, a lookout tower and a fortified tower dominating both the walled town and its citadel. Contemporary with the mosque at Kairouan, it superseded the Nador tower of the earlier ribat. A further possible influence could be the square tower of the early Christian monasteries of Coptic Egypt and of Palestine. Although the dates of construction of the Qasrs of the Egyptian desert monasteries are unknown with certainty, they were likely to have been incorporated into the monastery by the time the fortified minarets of Ifriqya were built. In addition Arab architects would almost certainly be aware of the defensive towers of the Palestinian monasteries.[6]

Finally mention must be made of the tall and richly decorated minarets of the western

---

[5] Stierlin (1996: 170) says that this form of minaret spread through North Africa to Spain from the 'Kutubiyya Mosque in Marakesh to the Giralda Tower of the Great Mosque of Seville'.

[6] The minaret continued to be used as a defensive tower into the fourteenth century. The 30m high tower of the White Mosque in Ramla, built in 1318 in the Holy Land, is provided with loopholes for archers. It is another mosque provided with cisterns under the courtyard, again from the Umayyad period. Hillenbrand (2000: 129–71) discusses at length the origin and function of the minaret, mentioning the role that the Umayyad Palace of Qasr al-Hair al-Gharbi may have played as a precursor of the mosque as 'a refuge for the faithful with the minaret as its bulwark'.

Maghreb that often reach a height of 65m. Syrian influence is again argued but this seems to be tenuous in the extreme. Many have a defensive look about them; small solitary entrances, windows which resemble loopholes and their sheer bulk, often up to 15m square, suggest a military purpose, although any suggestion of austerity or functionalism is removed by the remarkable patterned decoration. Access to the top of the minaret is via a ramp circling a square central core. Rabat and Marrakech in Morocco contain fine examples and the minaret at Tlemcen in Algeria is unique in having in its base the only entrance to the courtyard of the now destroyed mosque. The absence of rooms of any size and the ascent via the ramp around a central core argues against a military role, despite the visual statement of awesome power.

# Islamic monasticism and the khanaqah

Islamic monasticism took root, like its Christian originator, some time after the foundation of the religion by Muhammad; it was both eremetical and coenobitic. Almost all monasteries were built in urban areas and were as a consequence infrequently fortified. The rise of Sufism that first appeared in the late twelfth century saw the development of a new architectural form of Islamic monastery.

Sufism became a branch of Islam opposed to the more secular, structured and legal theology of orthodox Sunni Islam. Teaching a personal, mystical worship with Allah, it was influenced by Buddhism, Hinduism, and Persian Zoroastrianism. Surprisingly it incorporated some of the Christian beliefs of the monastic orders. There were, however, important differences between the monastic philosophies of the Christian monk and the Sufi mystic; he had, for example, no abbot, rather a teacher (shaikh) and the Sufi monastery could accommodate non-celibate pupils and devotees, although all led a simple, ascetic life of learning, prayer and charity. Like the later Western mendicant friars, many Sufis left their monasteries for significant periods and their khanaqahs offered shelter for specific groups of travellers. As a result many were built in rural areas and were thus more at risk of attack. It is not known, unlike with the ribat and the caravanserai, just how many were fortified. That some were fortified is demonstrated by two khanaqahs. One, the complex of **Jamal ad-Din** at Anau in Central Asia, has recently been severely damaged by an earthquake, the second, the khanaqah of **Pir Sadat** near Baku in Azerbaijan is identified by Hillenbrand as being fortified, enclosed as it is by a crenellated perimeter wall.[7] It is a trapezoidal fortified enclosure with round corner towers and semi-circular intermediary towers in the middle of three walls and a rectangular fortified gateway inserted into the fourth. In this respect it is not unlike the ribat of Sousse, although the Nador tower had been replaced by a minaret attached to one of the buildings lining the inner walls of the enceinte. To cater for the religious needs of the Sufis these buildings included a ceremonial hall, refectory, kitchen, library, cells and special quarters for guests and the shaikh. Its fame resulted in it developing into a pilgrimage site. The Sufis flourished under the Seljuks and many monasteries were built in Anatolia, Central Asia and Egypt. Unfortunately little attention has so far been paid to them.

[7] Hillenbrand (2000: 219–20).

# The multi-functional religious complex

Many of the problems posed in the study of Islamic architecture have already been discussed. The basic architectural template allows for easy change of use and function. Frequently buildings for differing functions were built contiguously; long-term building developments resulted in complexes that can be difficult to understand.

The previously mentioned khanaqah at Anau dates from the fifteenth century and was built within fortress walls. It became part of a complex that contained a mosque, a madrasa or collegiate mosque, literally a 'place of study', as well as lodgings for pilgrims.

The mosque at **Tinmal**, built in the tenth century in the High Atlas Mountains of Morocco, was fortified and became part of the fortifications of the nearby civil settlement. A mausoleum was added and for a time was deemed strong enough to serve as the State treasury and as a ribat, despite its modest size.

Somewhat similar in overall size, approximately 33 x 55m, is the irregular trapezoidal fortified complex of the **Chella** necropolis at Rabat, also in Morocco, that dates from the first half of the fourteenth century. Within the crenellated walls are sepulchral chambers, two mosques, minarets and a small monastery. There is a central court that leads to cells for the monastic residents. It has also been described as a ribat and played an important role in the jihad opposing the Spanish Reconquest. An interesting architectural feature is the solitary entrance gateway. The pointed archway is surrounded by decorative carving and flanked on either side by two semi-octagonal towers 15m tall surmounted by a square crenellated parapet. Both towers are loopholed at the level of the crenellated enceinte.

In Turkish Anatolia at **Kayseri** is the Khwand Khatun complex where a mosque and a madrasa are joined together. Both are protected by crenellated walls, interval towers and round corner towers. The courtyards are much reduced in size and there is a narrow solitary entrance to each, although the two communicate with each other internally. This is a unified fortified building serving two distinct but related functions.

# The citadel

It has been previously mentioned that, in the main, the Muslim populace preferred to defend itself by sheltering within walled towns and cities, with the ruling dynasties building within the walls their citadels whence they exercised their control and power.[8] Two such citadels, those of Cairo and Aleppo, warrant examination to understand the role of the mosque and minaret in such fortifications.

The Citadel of the Mountain overlooks the city of **Cairo** and the neighbouring city of Fustat; much of what remains dates from the twelfth century, when Saladin was instrumental in the building of many of the fortifications. It covers a huge area and comprises two irregularly shaped fortified enclosures. That to the north measures approximately 430m east to west and 250m north to south and served as the barracks and headquarters for the elite troops of the garrison. The southern enclosure, with its axis running north to south, is larger, measuring 480

---

[8] Hillenbrand (1999: 489–91).

x 280m, and contained the palaces and administrative buildings of the caliph or sultan. Both enclosures contain a number of mosques for the exclusive use of the different factions occupying the citadel; each regiment or corps of soldiers identified with a particular mosque. Chosen by Saladin for its strategic position, this was lost when the mosque of Sultan al-Hassan was built on high ground overlooking the citadel. Used by the Mamluks and more recently Napoleon, it served as an artillery bastion to bombard the citadel.

Much more dominating of its attached walled city is the citadel of **Aleppo**, built as it is on a prehistoric tell. This is a magnificent fortification, perching on the top of a steep glacis, surrounded by a ditch. The enceinte, oval in shape and measuring 500 x 350m, contains over forty square or rectangular towers and two barbicans. The main gate with its complex angled entrance is the finest example of Islamic fortification in Syria. Amongst the usual buildings of the citadel are two mosques. The Great Mosque, built by al-Zahir Ghazi and restored between 1213 and 1214 after a fire, has a tall and square minaret that served as a lookout tower for the citadel over the city and the surrounding countryside. The smaller mosque of the citadel was believed to be associated with the journeys made by Abraham and became a pilgrimage site as a result.

# The caravanserai and its relationship to the Hajj

Of all the Islamic buildings that both have religious connotations and can be deemed defensible or fortified, the most enduring, ubiquitous and numerous are the caravanserais, simply defined as rural fortified inns found along trade and pilgrimage routes. Whilst the Arab traders and merchants spread out from the Arabian peninsula in all directions, their caravans helping to sustain the far-flung garrisons and outposts, the greatest stimulus for travel was provided by the Hajj. One of the five Pillars of Islam, it is the duty of every believer to make, at least once in a lifetime, a pilgrimage to Mecca and the mosque of the Haram.[9] It is the most holy and sacred site in Islam, containing in the centre of a vast courtyard the Ka'ba, supposedly built by Abraham. For those who could not travel to Mecca, for whatever reason, lesser sites served to satisfy the need for the Baraka, or blessing.

Trade routes have existed since antiquity, and there has always been a concomitant need for shelter and protection of the merchants and their baggage animals that continued into the Byzantine and Sassanian eras. In the early days of the Arab conquests the victors had access to large pools of artisans and came into contact with many differing cultures; they quickly adapted to their needs those architectural forms necessary to maintain their empire. With the advent of the Dar al-Islam, the Abode of Peace, the role of the ribat and especially its military function lessened. Whilst travellers were unlikely to meet with aggressors from outside the empire, the vastness of their lands and the remoteness of many of the trade and pilgrimage routes necessitated protection from brigands and bandits who roamed the more isolated regions. In these regions an established ribat would be ideally suited for a change in use without much in

---

[9] The five Pillars of Islam are the Shahada. The belief that there is no God but God and Muhammad is the prophet of God, prayers five times daily, fasting from sunrise to sunset during the month of Ramadan, the giving of alms to the sick and poor and finally the Hajj.

the way of structural alterations.[10] However, not surprisingly, with any building which has been widely used throughout central Asia and the Middle East for over a thousand years, there is a wide variety of form and size, together with the number of services provided, although the basic Islamic structural template was followed. Travellers, whether merchants or pilgrims, needed shelter and sustenance, ideally at intervals of a day's journey.

The caravanserai at **Chah-i-Siyay**, near Isfahan in Iran, which dates from between 770 and 785, has a very similar ground plan to the two desert palace fortresses in Syria, as do the fortified inns between the Tigris and the Euphrates. The caravanserai, as well as occupying redundant ribats, architecturally probably originate from the early Syrian palaces; indeed there is a belief that the palaces east and west of Palmyra functioned as caravanserais.

Although heavily restored, the caravanserai built by Kayqubad I in 1229 between **Aksaray** and **Konya** is typical of many built in the thirteenth century in Turkish Anatolia. One of around a hundred such caravanserais, it has the distinct form of two rectangular adjoining and interconnecting buildings. This Seljuk caravanserai is larger than most and the smaller covered hall, measuring 31 x 50m, is attached to its larger courtyard (47.5 x 62.5m) containing the entrance gateway. Built of fine ashlar, unadorned externally, it is reinforced with semi-circular and faceted interval buttresses between the square and octagonal corner towers. The entrance gateway contains a muqamas vault that contrasts with the plain ashlar walls. This pointed recessed vault above the entrance arch is made up of small concave elements giving a honeycomb appearance and is surrounded by roundels and pillars carved with abstract patterns. The inner courtyard has arcaded porticoes built against the longest walls. They lead to small rooms used as workshops, a bath-house and private chambers. In the centre of this paved courtyard is a prayer room built on four arches, again richly carved with intertwined geometric patterns and roundels. The blank exterior is pierced only by rain spouts and high, narrow splayed loopholes, probably more for lighting than for defence. Although 12m high, the restored walls are devoid of crenellations, but the presence of a staircase suggests that there was a wall walk. Although there were twenty caravanserais on the 250km road between Kayseri and Konya, most caravanserais were built approximately 40km apart, the distance a camel can travel without food or water in a day.

## The pilgrimage caravanserai

At the other end of the spectrum is the **Khan al-Qutaifah** caravanserai in Syria, one of a group of sixteenth and seventeenth-century caravanserais built expressly for pilgrims. As Robert Hillenbrand states, it can be regarded as a 'miniature city', providing not only shelter and accommodation but also baths, restaurants, shops and a mosque.[11] The fortified enclosure wall measures 160 x 100m. The nineteenth-century caravanserai of **Aliabad**, on the Teheran to Qum highway in Persia represents perhaps the most sophisticated of any pilgrimage caravanserai and offers all that even the most privileged of pilgrims could want.

[10] Hillenbrand (2000: 341–2) discusses how the ribats of Central Asia changed roles when pacification made them redundant.

[11] Ibid. 352.

Many of these pilgrimage caravanserais were built by the rich and powerful of the day, not only as a service to Islam but in order to improve their standing both on earth and in paradise. The earliest such series, on the Baghdad to Mecca route where twenty caravanserais have been identified, was sponsored by the wife of Harun al-Rashid in the ninth century. Some three hundred years later the Seljuk sultan Malik-Shah, an implacable enemy of the Assassins, built a chain of caravanserais on the Hajj route from Mesopotamia to the holy cities. There is a similar chain between Antioch and Damascus that links up with those leading to Arabia.

As with most Islamic architecture there is a basic plan of a central courtyard surrounded by rooms for stabling and the storage of goods in transit, with lodging against a surrounding fortified enceinte entered by a single gate and fortified with round corner towers. This plan is followed from Afghanistan to the Middle East and Arabia; embellishments reflect only the richness of the patron or the importance of the pilgrim. Anatolian examples on the other hand would appear to be atypical in having an attached covered chamber.

## Ukhaidir, a fortified palace in Mesopotamia

Although a secular building the palace of **Ukhaidir** is worthy of inclusion as it is thought to have had a profound influence on both Eastern and Western ecclesiastical fortifications.

Located in what is now semi-arid countryside 120km south of Baghdad in Iraq, it was originally surrounded by a well-developed and fertile agricultural region when it was built around 778. The paranoia of its builder, Isa ibn-Musa, is shown by his need to surround his fortified palace, not yet completed, by a wall heavily fortified in a complex and innovative way. Constructed of rough-hewn mortared stone, this outer enceinte measures 174 x 170m and surrounds the rectangular palace. Its walls are approximately 19m high and 2.6m thick. The four gateways are each protected by flanking towers, a portcullis and guard-rooms and are found in the centre of each of the four walls. The main gate, in the north wall, is flanked by two square towers and leads directly into the palace in contrast to the other three entrances that open into a courtyard surrounding the palace through huge semi-circular projecting towers. The four circular corner towers contain a stairway leading to a barrel-vaulted and loopholed gallery that runs all the way round the enceinte widened by forty semi-circular towers linked by round-headed arch machicolations externally. The inner aspect of the wall is supported by square colonnaded buttresses solidly arched to further widen the walkway of this early chemin de ronde. This gallery is 4.5m wide and is splayed externally at intervals to produce loopholes and to give access to chambers in the upper part of the semi-circular buttresses. The gallery can also reached by staircases built either side of the south, east and west gates.

Whilst the palace, measuring 120 x 80m, is similarly surrounded by a buttressed wall, it is overlooked by the enclosure wall, and was, as a consequence indefensible once this outer wall was breached. It cannot therefore be considered a forerunner of the concentric castle. The similarity of this outer enceinte to those of the congregational or Friday mosques of Kufa and Samarra is, however, striking. This fortress palace is a very impressive example of sophisticated military architecture but the importance of this building lies in its machicolations.

Bonde is of the opinion that the fortress churches of the Languedoc, particularly Saint-

Pons-de-Thomières, have their closest parallels in the castle of the Crac des Chevaliers and Ukhaidir.[12] The way in which the arch machicolation came to be used in both secular and ecclesiastical fortifications in mediaeval Western Europe has never been chronologically traced. It is believed, however, that machicolations were used in ribats, since they are found in the existing ribats in Sousse and Monastir. In addition, the eleventh-century caravanserai of Ribat-i-Malik in Central Asia contains galleries. Both the Crusader castles of Saône incorporate these two forms of military architecture in their defences. Perhaps the Frankish military architects were introduced to the concept in the Islamic East and incorporated it in their castles. The frequent contacts between the south of France and the Holy Land suggest that the introduction of this novel and successful form of military architecture into Western Europe was inevitable.

[12] Bonde (1994: 141) points out that machicolations were used by the Roman, Byzantine and Islamic military engineers before arriving in Western Europe in the twelfth century.

# 16
# IRAN AND SYRIA

## Hasan-i-Sabah and the valley of Alamut

The journey made by Hasan-i-Sabah to the valley of Alamut in the Elburz Mountains of Iran, just to the south of the Caspian Sea, brought about an opposition to the established authority based entirely on fear and terror. Deeply religious since childhood, he converted to the Ismaili sect of Shiite Islam in 1072. As a result he became fanatically opposed to the Seljuk Turks who held power in the Middle East, after they had overcome the Shiite Abbasid dynasty in that part of the Islamic Empire that is present day Iran and Iraq. When adopting Islam, they had chosen to follow the orthodox Sunni faith.

Such was Hasan's opposition to the Seljuks and anybody professing Sunni Islam that he carefully planned the formation of a secret and revolutionary sect based upon Ismaili Shiite extremism. His first need was to establish a secure base from where he could carry out his campaign of revolutionary preaching and militancy. He sought a mountainous region where he could acquire or build castles to keep him and his followers safe from retribution and reprisal from the Seljuk Empire, preferably one with a disaffected population, sympathetic to extreme Shiite views, which could be converted or at least accept or tolerate them, and which was remote and inaccessible.

The people and the valleys of the Elburz Mountains appeared ideal for his purpose, and he earmarked the castle in the Alamut valley as his potential headquarters. Held on behalf of the ruling Seljuks, he acquired the castle by subterfuge after his Da'is, or missionaries, had begun the conversion of the garrison of the castle and its neighbouring villages.[1] Smuggled into the castle in disguise he was able to expel the Seljuk governor and begin to establish himself, his disciples and his cause in the valley of Alamut and its tributary and neighbouring valleys.

## The origins of the Ismaili sect of Islam

It is appropriate to digress at this point and consider the rise of the Ismaili Shiite sect following the great schism which occurred shortly after the death of Muhammad. Although he had unified the disparate and warring tribes of Arabia, he was not to see the start of their incredible conquests and the spread of Islam; rather his death plunged the Islamic world into turmoil. The 'Messenger of God', despite his religious fervour and organisational skills, had left no obvious successor.

Abu Bakr, father-in-law and one of the earliest and staunchest disciples of Muhammad, was chosen as the first caliph, or deputy of the Prophet. Right from the outset there were dissidents who wished Ali, the cousin and son-in-law of Muhammad, to succeed him and start

---

[1] A da'is, literally a summoner, preaching the message of the imam, the head of the Shiite community.

a bloodline, which was ultimately achieved in 656 when the third caliph was murdered. The mystical supporters of Ali belonged to the party of Ali, Shi'atu'Ali or simply Shia. Their strength was to remain in the Middle East, especially what is today Iran and part of Iraq.

The Orthodox or Sunni Muslims opposed the descendental doctrine of the Shiites and the murder in 680, of Hussein, the second son of Ali, who had been proclaimed caliph, saw the beginnings of 'Shiite martyrology with its strong streak of esotericism and thirst for revenge'.[2]

The Shiites were not to remain unified for long; in the eighth century there was a split between the moderates and the extremists after the death of the sixth imam, the religious leader of the Shiites. His eldest son Isma'il was disinherited, possibly due to his association with the militants who sought power by force, and his younger brother became the seventh imam. Those Shiites who remained loyal to Isma'il formed a breakaway sect, the Ismailis.

The complexities of the rivalries between the Sunnis and the Shiites need not concern us here, nor the ebb and flow of Ismaili power, except to record a further schism in 1094, this time amongst the Ismailis. Nizar, the appointed heir to the Shiite caliph of Egypt, al-Mustansir, was displaced in favour of his brother. Attempting to gain the caliphate by force of arms, Nizar was captured and put to death, with the result that many eastern Shiites preferred henceforth to follow the line of Nizar.

It was to this sect that Hasan-i-Sabah gave his lifetime powers of devotion, allegiance and leadership. Pockets of Nizari Ismailis were to be found throughout Persia but in order for Hasan to carry out his mission he required a more secure base than his devotees could supply in the cities. His first need was to consolidate his occupancy of the Elburz Mountains, acquire new converts, and capture, buy or build more castles to accommodate his followers. Only then could he form his secret and murderous band of soldier disciples, the Fida'iin, known to the Crusaders as Assassins.

## The Assassins

Hasan's cause was made easier by the alienation, resulting from the Seljuk conquest, of many revolutionary zealots, who were happy to accept his preaching and live in his mountain fastness. Legends abound on the methods Hasan employed to convert numbers of his followers into a disciplined, trained, blindly obedient and self-sacrificing body of killers, who would murder, without question, at his bidding. Even their name adds to these legends. The word 'assassin' is believed to be a derivative of 'hashish', a drug reputedly used by Hasan and his instructors in the training of their killers, the Fida'iin. It was used as one of the ways of inculcating into the minds of the Fida'iin the notion that entry into Paradise would be the reward for dying for the cause of the Nizari Ismailis. Chosen to become a political killer for the avowed revolutionary aim of overthrowing the Seljuks and removing orthodox Sunni Islam from power, the Assassin expected to die when carrying out his orders.

Hasan had travelled widely through the countries of Islam for many years before he arrived at Alamut. Legend states that he built there a garden so beautiful that it recalled

---

[2] Pean (1995: introduction).

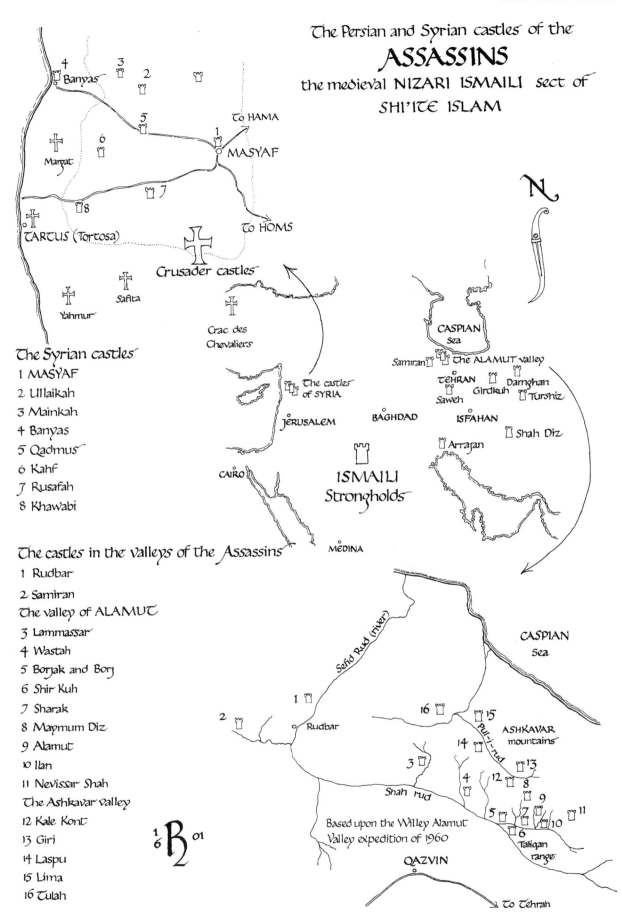

The Persian and Syrian castles of the
# ASSASSINS
the medieval NIZARI ISMAILI sect of
SHI'ITE ISLAM

4 Banyas
3
2
To HAMA
5
1
MASYAF
6
Margat
7
8
TARTUS (Tortosa)
To HOMS
Crusader castles
Safita
Yahmur
Crac des Chevaliers

The castles of SYRIA
JERUSALEM
BAGHDAD
CAIRO
ISMAILI Strongholds
MEDINA

N

CASPIAN Sea
Samiran  The ALAMUT valley
TEHRAN  Damghan
Saweh  Girdkuh  Turshiz
ISFAHAN
Arrajan  Shah Diz

## The Syrian castles
1 MASYAF
2 Ullaikah
3 Mainkah
4 Banyas
5 Qadmus
6 Kahf
7 Rusafah
8 Khawabi

## The castles in the valleys of the Assassins
1 Rudbar
2 Samiran
The valley of ALAMUT
3 Lammassar
4 Wastah
5 Borjak and Borj
6 Shir Kuh
7 Sharak
8 Maymum Diz
9 Alamut
10 Ilan
11 Nevissar Shah
The Ashkavar valley
12 Kale Kont
13 Giri
14 Laspu
15 Lima
16 Tulah

CASPIAN Sea
Sefid Rud (river)
1
2  Rudbar
16  15
Pul-i-rud  ASHKAVAR mountains
14
3  13
4  12  8
Shah rud  9
5  7
Based upon the Willey Alamut
Valley expedition of 1960
6
10  11
Taliqan range
QAZVIN
To Tehran

1601 B2

Paradise, representing as closely as possible the Qur'anic description of Paradise as a 'garden flowing with streams'. Living in this wondrous garden were the most beautiful of women. It is easy to understand the impression this earthly notion of Paradise would have made on those schooled by the master into his beliefs, who were susceptible to his will and suggestion, especially if hallucinogenic drugs were used. Other legends encourage the belief that Hasan started to train his Fida'iin from an early age. Taught the language and culture of those whom he believed were his enemies, the Assassin would be able to get near his intended victim without arousing suspicion.

Whatever the method used, Hasan surrounded himself with a substantial number of fanatics, sworn to absolute secrecy, total loyalty and blind obedience. So persuasive was the master that he had no shortage of volunteers prepared to carry out ritualistic murder, always with a jambiya, the curved dagger favoured by Arabs.

The Assassin was almost always caught and killed, indeed he welcomed death as it gave him the opportunity to enter Paradise, the ultimate reward for the fanatic. Hasan even set up in his castle a 'role of honour' where the name of the Fida'i, that of his victim and his position in society were recorded. Once Hasan entered the castle of the Alamut valley he became reclusive and spent his last thirty five years living a celibate and ascetic life, all the while planning his reign of terror, based upon the assassination of those Seljuk and other leaders who opposed him and sought to harm his cause.

The victims were always selected with the utmost care; those actively hostile to the Ismailis were most at risk, as were those who had harmed this secret sect. No one was immune, whether caliph, minister or army commander; indeed the threat or deed of assassination of garrison commanders in castles coveted by the Ismailis was an effective way of gaining control.

## The castles of the valleys of Alamut

As Lewis states, the Ismaili strategy was one of 'penetration, entrenchment and attack'.[3] The Ismailis acquired their castles and built others together with linking towers and small outworks to produce a consolidated defensive network, as the examination of the remains in **Alamut** will show.

There were small outposts of the sect in other mountainous regions of Persia, for example in the south-west between Kuzistan and Fars and in Quhistan, the mountainous region between Persia and Afghanistan; unfortunately there are scant remains of castles and no studies available. What little knowledge we have of the castles of Alamut is a result of an expedition led by Peter Willey into the mountains of Elburz in 1960. His expedition faced many difficulties in identifying and surveying the castles, not least because of the destruction meted out by the Mongols, subsequent earthquakes and later overbuilding.

From what little information we have on the Assassin castles of Persia and Syria it is possible to make a number of generalisations about the Ismaili castles. All are to be found in mountainous regions where there was a disaffected population with Shiite traditions. They are interdependent and linked visually with a number of lookout towers, providing an intricate

---

[3] Lewis (1985: 44).

system of signalling: sited, where possible, on rocky outcrops they overlook valleys fertile enough to maintain the garrisons and the dependant villages and towns of the Ismaili sympathisers. The garrison commander was a celibate ascetic and his warriors led an almost monastic existence. The castles were large enough to shelter all the members of the sect during times of threat, and contained stores and cisterns to enable them to resist a substantial siege. The military architecture almost certainly reflected localised development; rough-coursed stone is used in conjunction with brick, bound with a clay mortar. Access was always difficult, with only tracks for the pack animals used to supply the castles.

Huge cisterns were needed, not only to supply the castle but also to feed the irrigation system required to water the gardens and cultivated fields in the dry environment of summer. Channels from the extensive rocky catchment areas led to cisterns both inside and outside the castle so arranged as to enable any overflow to be channelled into another cistern. One of the cisterns in the castle of Lammassar still retains the post holes used to support a roof or awning to prevent evaporation. The garrison was able to draw water by two means from the river that ran below its walls. One of the towers of the enceinte was built to overhang the river and water could be obtained by lowering a bucket from a trap door, and a tunnel, hewn from rock and guarded by a tower, ran from the castle for some two hundred metres down to the river.[4]

Hasan planned his mountain citadel carefully and ensured that strategically placed castles controlled all access routes into his heartland. The valley is some 40km long and in places 25km wide; bounded by mountain ranges up to 3000m high on the north, south and east, the western entrance is through the narrow gorge of Shir Kuh. Hasan built a castle here with two outlying forts either side of the river and protected the eastern approach with the castles of Ilan and Nevisar Shah. The large castle of Maymum Diz protected any approach from mountain passes to the north, whilst the large castle of Lammassar protected any approach from the valley of the Shah River (Rud). This fortified mountain valley, the centre of Naziri Ismaili power, was further protected by an outer ring of castles and fortifications. The Seljuks were aware of what was happening and sent an army to capture the valley in 1092, which was not only repulsed but was to herald the first of the murderous attacks on those in power who opposed the Ismailis. Nizam al-Mulk, the grand vizier who had orchestrated the attack on Alamut, was murdered by one of Hasan's Fida'iin disguised as a Sufi to gain access.

# The castle of Alamut and the 'garden of streams'

**Alamut** was home to Hasan all his life and it is probable that if his legendary garden did exist it was located here. Willey and his party spent some time at this castle and his findings are interesting, although the interpretation below is speculative. The castle dates from the middle of the ninth century and was probably built by religious refugees from the Abbasid caliphs. Altered and extended by Hasan after he acquired it around 1090, it was destroyed by the Mongols after it fell into their hands in 1258. Rebuilt during the Safavid Persian dynasty (1502–1736), it was used as a royal prison in the seventeenth and eighteenth centuries before falling into ruins again. Strongly sited, the castle is in two parts and although there are sizeable

[4] Willey (1963: 274).

remains of the fortifications these are probably Persian additions. What is interesting and almost certainly from the time of Hasan is a qanat or water channel of gigantic proportions. Measured by Willey's team at some 200m long, with a width of 4m and similar in depth, he found evidence of attempted destruction, possibly by the Mongols. Running east to west across the southern slope of the eastern part of the castle, it is reached by rock cut steps from the castle above. An obvious reservoir for the collection of rain water from the rocky slopes above, its position may be explained by the utilisation of a natural rocky fault during its excavation. There are no associated fortifications with this qanat, making it unlikely that it was primarily a cistern in case of siege, particularly as both parts of the castle contained cisterns within their walls. Alternative theories suggest that it may be a reservoir either to serve the neighbouring villagers or to provide water for the irrigation of their fields. Willey feels that it was both a moat and a water channel. Whilst it was not possible to tell where the qanat led to westwards, the eastern end led to the north-eastern extremity of the second or 'onion' castle, so named because of the bulbous rock which rises above the ridge. This part of the castle is oval in shape, measuring 300 x 200m, and defended by cliffs to the north and east. The south-western aspect is cut off by a wall from the qanat and the whole area was found to contain many clay water pipes, unfortunately so disturbed that any water distribution scheme could not be identified. That the qanat served as the reservoir needed to supply the 'Garden of Streams' is, perhaps, more fanciful than the prosaic view of it functioning as a moat or as part of an irrigation system for the fields necessary to supply the castle.[5]

Willey and his team found other castles where sophisticated water collecting and distributing systems still remain. At Shir Kuh, the collecting system almost rivals that of Alamut; situated at the entrance to the valley it is not only smaller but more vulnerable. Interestingly these reservoirs and overflow channels are again outside the defences of the castle. At the castle of Lammassar there is a catchment area which drains into cisterns, again connected by channels to drain away overflow. Earthenware conduit pipes were again discovered.[6] Neither castle has any reservoir or channel approaching the size of the qanat at Alamut, however; as all the castles are so ruinous it is unsafe to draw any conclusions.

## Expansion of the Assassins into Syria

The success achieved by Hasan in organising his extremist revolutionary state in Alamut, together with other enclaves in Persia, allowed the Ismailis not only to challenge the might of the Seljuks and the orthodoxy of the Sunnis, but also to have the confidence to establish a colony in Syria. The arrival of the Crusaders and the capture of Jerusalem in 1099 together with the decline of the Shiite Fatimid Empire in Egypt had resulted in political and religious instability in the Near East. Coinciding with reverses for the Ismaili cause in Aleppo and Damascus, the Da'is now turned their attention to the mountainous region of the Jabal Bahra between the city of Hama and the Eastern Mediterranean coast, in present-day Syria.

The instructions from Alamut were very simple: to follow the tried and tested formula of

---

[5] Ibid. 214–24.
[6] Ibid. 257 and 274.

securing, by whatever means, a number of castles in a remote and inaccessible region, where the indigenous population were receptive to the Ismaili preachers and missionaries. Progress was slow at first, in acquiring either converts or castles, but by 1141 they had managed to obtain **Qadmus**, bought in 1132 from its Muslim ruler, Khariba. Previously garrisoned by Frankish Crusaders who had been driven out by the Ismailis between 1136 and 1137, it had returned to Muslim care. Similarly, **Masyaf** Castle, captured from the Seljuks around 1140, was destined to become the most important of the Assassin castles in Syria and the 'mother of Assassin frontier castles'.[7]

The acquisition of these castles together with the fearsome reputation that the Ismailis had achieved resulted in little attempt to counter their threat, let alone attempt to dislodge them, by either orthodox Muslims or Christian Crusaders who surrounded them on all sides. As Runciman comments 'the appearance of a new and disruptive sect would hinder a Muslim counter-Crusade' and could be of use to the Crusaders, especially as the Assassins did not change the direction of their policies; Seljuk and Sunni were the implacable enemies, not the Christian Crusader.[8]

## The arrival of Sinan, the 'Old Man of the Mountains'

During the middle years of the twelfth century more converts were attracted to the valleys and more castles built. It was, however, the arrival of Sinan, a leader of exceptional abilities, that was to result in the firm establishment of this dependency of Alamut. This small revolutionary state, encompassing an area of less than a thousand square kilometres, was to have an influence out of all proportion to its size. It was something of a buffer state, being surrounded to the south, west and north by the Crusader county of Tripoli and the principality of Antioch and to the east by the Sunni Muslim state of Damascus. It was, however, fiercely independent.

Sinan, born Rashid al-Din into an important family of Basra, now in Iraq, entered the valley of Alamut as a youth following a family rift. His abilities were soon recognised and, along with the sons of the Ismaili leadership, he received Nizari indoctrination and a military and political education.[9] He was ordered to Syria after a short spell as a missionary in his own town, and soon consolidated the Ismaili position in its small mountain enclave, capturing the castle of Ullaikah and rebuilding Rusafah and Khawabi. As at Alamut the castles became part of a defensive military complex with a sophisticated communications system using carrier pigeons, protecting the settlements of the believers in the fertile valleys. Realising his precarious and vulnerable position, especially as he had no army of any size to oppose the Sunnis or defend against Crusader raids, he followed the ways of the Alamut leadership in using fear and politics to ensure the survival of his beleaguered emirate. His immediate task was to choose the most able, devoted and fanatical of his followers to train as his Fida'iin, men who would defend the Ismaili cause without question.[10]

[7] Hillenbrand (1999: 501).
[8] Runciman (1965a: 119).
[9] Lewis (1985: 110–11) quotes the biographer of Sinan.
[10] Mirza (1997: 27–8).

Sinan was to rule his Syrian enclave until his death around 1193, initially with Alamut as suzerain, although Alamut's control and influence waned as Sinan became more powerful and autocratic. He was widely known in the West and amongst the Crusaders as the 'Old Man of the Mountains', but this sobriquet was never used by the Nizari Ismailis, to whom he remained the revered representative of the imam.[11] Described by a contemporary Sunni writer as 'a man of knowledge, statecraft and skill in winning men's hearts' he followed the Alamut leadership in using his Fida'iin to achieve his aims, his ordered assassinations included high-ranking Christians.[12] The continuing existence of this small but independent state depended upon its isolation and inaccessibility, the political skills of its leaders, the connivance of the Crusaders and the fear engendered by the sinister Fida'iin.

The Old Man of the Mountains became synonymous with the successors of Sinan and is frequently mentioned in Crusader journals. Joinville, who wrote about the crusade of St Louis IX, king of France, describes graphically the power and megalomania of the Syrian Nizari leader as he travelled round his domains. Preceded by a carrier bearing an axe studded with knives, the population is repeatedly exhorted to 'turn out of the way of Him who bears in his hands the death of kings!'[13]

## The castles

The castles of the Assassins in Syria, like their counterparts in Persia, are now so ruined that in almost every case even the ground plan is barely discernible. So ruinous are the structures above ground that only **Masyaf** today can be instantly recognised as a castle. A visitor to the coastal town of Tortosa in 1212, Wilbrand of Oldenburg, remarked of the Crusader castle of Margat that 'opposed to it are many strong castles of the Old Man of the Mountain'.[14] When T. E. Lawrence visited the region in 1908 he was singularly unimpressed, and almost scathing in describing the Assassin castles of Qadmus and Masyad (Masyaf) as 'absurdly weak'.[15] As Smail points out, however, the best defence of a castle is its inaccessibility and the use made of natural features.[16] Sinan sited his castles well, choosing precipitate rocky outcrops and mountain crests, close enough with their attendant towers and fortlets to form a composite, intervisible and interdependent whole, much in the way Hasan did in and around Alamut. There were no castles here to rival Margat or the Crac des Chevaliers, yet few attempts were made to capture the castles until the final days of the Assassins.

The castles dominated remote and fertile river valleys. Eight can be identified with certainty and another three or four as temporary citadels for the Ismailis. Unlike Alamut, no

[11] Kennedy (1994: 166). Mention of the Old Man of the Mountains is made by Wilbrand of Oldenburg, a German traveller, who visited the castle of Crac des Chevaliers in 1212. According to Boase (1967: 75), he also wrote 'who is wont through his messengers to kill our men with daggers'.

[12] Mirza (1997: 39).

[13] Joinville and Villehardouin (1963: 280).

[14] Boase (1967: 75).

[15] Lawrence (1988: 350).

[16] Smail (1995: 217).

one castle can be identified as the domicile of the Grand Master, the Syrian leadership preferring to move from one castle to another. The historian and archbishop William of Tyre estimated that Sinan had 60,000 followers in his mountain fastness by the second half of the twelfth century, living in villages and townships sheltering in the lee of the castles, each settlement having an agricultural, trading and economic infrastructure. Castles, as at Alamut, were only occupied in times of danger. It has been postulated that the Ismaili castles were populated by whole communities of the followers of the Old Man. But whilst some of the Alamut castles were large enough to do so those in Syria are simply not large enough to accommodate a small township of 700–800 persons together with their material possessions (William of Tyre's figures).[17]

**Masyaf**, standing atop a hillock, is the best preserved of the castles; surrounded by its present-day village, it retains its walls but is now a castle of many different building periods.[18] The multi-towered outer wall and gatehouse surrounds a dominating inner keep-like fortified enclosure. There is little space here to accommodate a civilian farming and merchant population on top of the ruling hierarchy, its teachers, missionaries and trainee Fida'iin, except in time of danger, although it almost certainly had a different ground plan when first built.

Destruction of the Assassins' castles is so great that only a few generalisations can be made. All are built of rough-hewn stone. Most contain mosques, baths and cisterns, and some still have the remains of a water-distribution system by means of clay pipes. Nearly all have a solitary eastern gateway reached by a flight of stairs. Apart from Masyaf, only one, Ullaikah, built on a spur of the Taraz Mountains in the direction of Damascus, is anything other than a simple enclosure castle. It has two walls, one within the other and thus appears to have been a concentric castle containing all the features of these castles. Many have now been built over, masking any remaining features, and they have, in the main, not been examined by archaeologists.[19]

# The relationship between the Assassins and the Crusaders

Prior to their settlement in the Syrian Mountains, the Ismailis in Aleppo carried out a number of assassinations of Seljuks and Sunni Muslims, two of which were of particular value to the Crusaders. The murder of the emir of Apamea in 1106 was of benefit to Tancred, the prince of Antioch. The assassination of Mawdud, the emir of Mosul, in 1113, who was the leader of an expeditionary force assembled to help the Syrian Muslims against the Crusaders, removed a powerful enemy of the Franks. Crusader dialogue with Ridwan, the Muslim ruler of Aleppo, would have informed them of his patronage of this fundamentalist sect, so bitterly opposed to the enemies of the Christians. It is not too surprising therefore that when Ridwan died, thus removing protection of the Assassins in Aleppo, they sought refuge in Crusader-controlled

---

[17] This may have been the case at Subeibe Castle, near Banyas in Syria, the first stronghold acquired by the Persian Ismailis in 1126, but which was evacuated within two to three years.

[18] Müller-Wiener (1966: 68) describes the castle as an 'extremely compact citadel'.

[19] Hanna (1994: 101).

country.[20] The sect went underground and started to acquire castles, which could only have been achieved with the support and connivance of the Franks, who believed that they had little to fear and much to gain from the bitter enemies of the Seljuks and Sunnis. Little is known of the early relationship between Crusader and Assassin, although Raymond of Antioch was in an alliance with an Assassin chief in 1148 and in 1152 Count Raymond II was murdered by Fida'iin at the southern gateway into Tripoli, an act where the motive remains unknown.[21] Tribute had been paid to the Templars at Tortosa and in 1173 the sectarians under the leadership of Sinan felt strong enough to suggest an alliance with Amalric, the king of Jerusalem, against Nur al-Din, the chief enemy of the Christians, in return for the cessation of this tribute.

This was the time of Saladin, who was embarking on his campaign to rid the Holy Land of all Crusaders; the Assassins sided with the opponents of Saladin, whether Christian or Muslim. So antagonistic was the Old Man of the Mountains to Saladin that he twice sent his Fida'iin to assassinate him. Both attempts were unsuccessful and Saladin responded by entering the territory of the Assassins and laying siege to Masyaf, only to lift it after a short time. Although it is chronicled that the siege ended when Saladin woke one morning to find an Assassin's dagger at the side of his bed together with a poem that warned of the consequences of his campaign against the Ismailis, the truth is likely to be more prosaic. The army had had enough of campaigning, had acquired sufficient booty, and wished to return to Egypt. The upshot was an apology to the Old man of the Mountains and a treaty that endured.[22]

Whilst nobody was immune to the Assassins' blade, few Christians were targeted by the Ismailis, in stark contrast to the Sunnis. The murder of Conrad of Montferrat, king of the Latin Kingdom of Jerusalem in April 1192, demonstrated the planning and stealth of the Assassins. The piety and sincerity showed by two of Sinan's devotees in wishing to convert to Christianity was so convincing that Conrad was prepared to sponsor their baptism and as a consequence they had no difficulty in approaching Conrad when Sinan gave his order. The murder was apparently in revenge for an act of piracy ordered by Conrad on one of the merchant ships of the sect and his subsequent refusal to return its goods and the crew. Others postulate that Saladin paid Sinan to assassinate both Conrad and Richard Lionheart, Richard being spared as the murder of two senior Crusader leaders may have led the way open for Saladin to renege on his treaty with the sect and thus reopen hostilities.[23]

Despite paying tribute to them, the Christian military orders were not targeted. The Assassins were of the opinion that the exercise would be futile, since to assassinate a Grand Master would serve no purpose; he would immediately be replaced by a successor of equal merit and there would be no destabilisation of the orders. Such, however, were Crusader politics that the assassination of Raymond, the eldest son of Bohemond IV of Antioch in the cathedral at Tortosa in 1213, followed shortly afterwards by Patriarch Albert of Jerusalem, was believed to have been instigated by the Hospitallers.[24] Bohemond sought his revenge against the Assassins by besieging, with Templar support, the Ismaili castle of Khawabi. Further use of the Assassins by the Hospitallers for their own ends resulted in the murder of Adam Baghras, regent of Christian Armenian Cilicia. The payment of tribute obviously rankled with the

---

[20] Runciman (1965a: 127).    [21] Ibid. 325–6 and 333.
[22] Ibid. 410.    [23] Runciman (1965b: 65).    [24] Ibid. 138.

Ismailis, although they were happy to receive it from both Christian and Muslim leaders fearful of the threat of assassination. Joinville, senechal to the French king and Crusader, St Louis, records that amongst others, tribute was paid by the emperor of Germany, the king of Hungary and the sultan in Cairo to ensure 'the friendship of the Old Man of the Mountains'.[25]

Despite the annihilation of the Persian Ismailis and the threat from Sultan Baybars, ultimately to bring about their downfall, the Syrian Ismailis showed their gratitude when victories over the Christians removed the need to pay tribute to the Hospitallers. The assassination of Philip of Montfort in Tyre in 1270, followed by the attempt on the life of Prince Edward of England in 1272, was a desperate attempt by the Ismailis to stave off their demise. They also offered help to Baybars during his siege and capture of the Hospitaller castle of Crac des Chevaliers, a further attempt to survive the inevitable.

# The final years

The Mongol advance through Persia and the fall of Baghdad in the middle of the thirteenth century resulted in the whole of Persia falling under the control of the Great Khan, with the exception of the Ismaili castles in the north. Despite years of negotiation, the Ismailis were unable to reach an agreement with these invaders from the East and the leadership became divided amongst itself, some wanting to resist, others wishing to obtain the best terms they could. Hulegu Khan, commander in chief of the Mongol army and grandson of the great Genghis, had only the destruction of the Ismailis in mind. This heretical sect that had resisted all attempts to destroy it was now facing its greatest threat as the Mongol army entered the mountain stronghold. Castle after castle tendered its surrender, only the commanders of Alamut and Lammassar refusing. The Mongol response was to besiege both, Alamut surrendering within a few days, Lammassar holding out for two years until 1258. All the castles were reduced and made untenable, their occupants put to the sword. The power the sect had held in Persia was over for good.[26]

The Syrian branch, well aware of what had happened in Alamut, had sought to ally itself with Baybars, the Mamluk sultan of Egypt who was liberating the Holy Land from the Crusaders and intending to oppose the Mongol invasion. Recognising the threat that the Assassins posed, Baybars rejected any alliance and sent a force into the Jabal Bahra to besiege those castles that refused to surrender. Ullaikah, Rusafah, and Khawabi fell in 1271, although the others held out to differing degrees. By 1273 all the castles were under the control of Baybars; the power of the sect had been destroyed for ever.

This extremist sect, which gave the word assassin to the English language, had for almost two hundred years led a revolutionary campaign against the Seljuks, Sunni Muslims and anybody who opposed them, using murder and the threat of murder. Their campaign of terror pervaded the whole of the Middle East, and with their perverse belief that assassination was a legitimate way to achieve their aims, they were universally loathed as well as feared. In the end this was all they achieved.

[25] Joinville and Villehardouin (1963: 277).
[26] Lewis (1985: 94–6).

# THE HIMALAYAN REGION

## The Tibetan cultural region

Tibet, that remote, mysterious and little-known country, spiritual if no longer temporal home to the Dalai Lama, has kept alive a way of life and a rich and ancient culture, irrevocably intertwined with the magical and mystical form of Tantric Buddhism. Its basis is compassion and wisdom, manifesting itself in the gentleness of the Tibetan people, the devotions of the legions of crimson-robed monks and the splendour of those ubiquitous seats of learning and repositories of knowledge, thought and philosophy, the monasteries. Unfortunately, huge numbers were so cynically and wantonly damaged or destroyed by the Red Guards of the Chinese Cultural Revolution during the 1960s.

Sandwiched between India and China, the awesome Himalayas hold back the inhospitable and arid Jang Tang, the Tibetan plateau known to its inhabitants as the 'Roof of the World'. This physical environment, the adoption for the second time of Buddhism in the eleventh century and a self-imposed isolation has produced a culture of intrigue that has spread beyond its geographical boundaries. Indeed, it is better to consider a Tibetan cultural world as its people, religion, art, literature and architecture have spread to China in the east, and Bhutan, Sikkim, Nepal and the Indian Himalayas to the south and west.

Tantric Buddhism pervades all aspects of life in Tibet and the Himalayan regions, with the exception of the southern reaches of Nepal, and everywhere are to be found monasteries, tangible expressions of Buddhist power and the hold it has on a deeply religious people.

Whilst the primary concern is with the fortified monasteries that were built from the fifteenth century onwards in the Himalayas, central Tibet, the eastern province of Kham and neighbouring China, an understanding of the origin and development of the various sects is required. Intense rivalries, political machinations and religious intrigue ensured that the Tibetan region remained in solitary limbo, its population serfs to the secular nobility and the powerful monastic lamas until the middle of the twentieth century.

### The origins of Tibetan Buddhism

The Buddhist Dharma, or teachings, were proclaimed by Sidhartha Gautama, an Indian prince from the north-east of the country who renounced his wealth and status, and turned to a life as an ascete in the sixth century BC. Announced as the first Buddha, his philosophies and the preaching of his missionaries were slow to reach the Himalayas and did not penetrate into Tibet until almost a thousand years after his death.

These early missionaries had to confront the local deities and their priesthood, which they successfully did by incorporating these powerful Tibetan deities into Buddhist theology, transforming them into protectors of the Dharma. This conversion occurred around the time Tibet was becoming united in the seventh century by King Songtsen Gampo, the son of the warlord of Yarlung. Using his military skills he conquered vast tracts of land. His hold was further strengthened by his shrewd marriage to Chinese and Nepalese princesses who were both devout Buddhists, thus making the task of his missionaries easier. Government was centralised in the Lhasa region, where he built his palace on the site of the present Potala Palace. The power of Tibet increased over the next two centuries and the empire extended into present-day Kashmir, Nepal, Sikkim, Bhutan, upper Burma and western China. The Indian Tantric master Padmasambhava was invited into Tibet by King Trisong Detsan, who had ascended to the throne in 815, and there was consequently a change in approach to the mix of ancient Indian Buddhism and the worship of indigenous Tibetan deities. In trying to enforce a strictly orthodox Buddhism, he engendered such hostility that he was assassinated and his Yarlung empire descended into civil war, the resulting disintegration leading to the establishment of small warring kingdoms throughout the Tibetan ethnic region.

One such kingdom, that of Guge, roughly approximating to western Tibet and the Ladakh region of Kashmir in the Indian Himalayas, is believed to have initiated the re-establishment of Buddhism by inviting in 1042 the great Indian master Ringchen Zangpo, who then travelled on to Tibet. Tibetan scholars had sporadically travelled to India to obtain and translate texts; however, it was Zangpo's mastery of the Tibetan language which stimulated the assimilation of Indian Buddhist texts and the reaffirmation of Buddhism as the religion of Tibet.

Contacts with India continued until the Islamic invasion and conquest of north India saw the total destruction of the great Indian Buddhist centres. The last was Vikramshila, in the early thirteenth century, a centre much visited by Tibetan scholars. The influence of Indian Buddhism and culture now ceased. Indian art had long been assimilated and adapted to local needs and traditions. Architecture was entirely Tibetan in origin; development and building styles derive from the trans-Himalayan house, although Indian monastic layout initially influenced Tibetan religious architecture. Monastic content developed a settled format, typically Tibetan in style with adaptation according to local needs or position. A relationship developed with military architecture either by fusion or spatial arrangement.[1]

The early Tibetan Empire had used the advent of Buddhism to establish and maintain control of its frontiers. Whilst the power base was in central Tibet, links with India had provided the kings of central Tibet, and later those of Guge, with a sophisticated military machine: better armaments and the use of proven tactics ensured that the opposing tribal warrior coalitions were at a distinct disadvantage. As Hosla points out, the acquisition of new territory was planned around a military and civil administration centred on a fort and the nearby monastery.[2] The monastery was to become 'an extension of the political arm of the king' playing a vital role in the conversion of tribal rituals and festivals into Buddhist ones, at the same time introducing literacy, education, local government and commerce. There are scant archaeological remains identified from this period. It is claimed that despite the ravages of civil war, earthquake, fires and more recently, the depredations of the Red Guards, the central Tibetan monastery of Samye dates from the later part of the eighth century. The nearby

[1] Tucci (1967: 111–15).
[2] Hosla (1979: 76).

fortress of Yumbu Lagang, reputedly the oldest dwelling in Tibet, is earlier, dating from the seventh century.

Founded by King Trisong Detsen, **Samye** was the first monastery to be established in Tibet and has its buildings arranged in the shape of a mandala to represent Buddhist cosmology. There are today no identifiable remains of the neighbouring castle or fort, the seat of power of the local nobility and the garrison commander.

**Yumbu Lagang** reaches into the skies from its rocky mountain pinnacle overlooking a fertile and well-populated river plain. Totally destroyed recently by the Chinese, it has now been completely rebuilt. Now the seat of a small monastery, its multi-storey tower was, perhaps, the forerunner of many of the lookout towers that dot the mountain tops of central and western Tibet. Ascent by foot is difficult and its high walls would make scaling difficult.

### The influence of the Mongols

The Himalayas had protected the Tibetan region from the influence of Islam. A new threat, however, appeared in the north-east, where Genghis Khan, who had by 1206 united all the nomadic tribes of Mongolia, was about to embark on his last, and most terrible, conquest. The Tibetans were aware of the nature of Mongol invasion; all opposition was crushed without mercy. Submission without any opposition to the Mongol raiding parties of 1239 saved Tibet from the severe depredations that the Mongols inflicted upon regions that resisted conquest. As a consequence Tibet became part of the empire of the Great Khan, an event of significance in the development of Buddhism since Kublai Khan, the grandson of Genghis, embraced Buddhism in 1270 and became a powerful and generous patron.

His conquest of the Sung Empire of China in 1279 resulted in Mongol support that was both protective and financial. It was the start of that peculiar relationship between China and Tibet known as Yon-Mchod, or Patron and Priest; the Chinese emperor and the chief lama each exerted an influence over the other. Tibet became once again a political entity with the core revolving around the Yarlung–Lhasa–Shigatse region of central Tibet in the fourteenth century.

### The rise of the sects and the ascendancy of the Gelukpas

The original school of Tibetan Buddhism, based on the early Indian teachings, became known as the Nyingmapa, or Red Hat sect founded by Guru Rimpoche (Padmasambhava), whose first monastery was at Samye. By the end of the eleventh century, Tibetan isolation, introspection and the obsession with Buddhist theology led to the formation of two further lineages: the Kagyupa and the Sakyapa. The former introduced the incarnate-lama system of succession and played a great part in the formation of the present kingdom of Bhutan, whilst the later, continuing with a hereditary approach, became increasingly powerful as a result of its influence upon, and favours received from, the ruling Mongolian aristocracy. The head lama of the Sakyapa had by the thirteenth century become the most powerful man in Tibet with a role as spiritual mentor and teacher to the Buddhist emperor of China.

By the late fourteenth century, however, his power had been substantially eroded by the rise to prominence of a reformist movement led by Je Rinpoche, better known as Tsongkhapa. His Gelukpa, or Yellow Hat, order rapidly eclipsed the Red Hats and became the most powerful and largest of all the schools of Tibetan Buddhism. The incarnate Dalai and Panchen Lamas belong to the Gelukpa school, and it is from these Yellow Hats that Tibet developed the theocracy resulting in this priestly order, through the office of the Dalai Lama, taking political control of Tibet.[3]

The rise to prominence of the Yellow Hats was not a peaceful one, and whilst the two rival sects differed little in basic theology, the Red Hats were not prepared to lose power to the Gelukpas. Both groups sought to ally themselves to the Tibetan nobility and the Mongolian overlords to the north. It was a time of 'bitter, bloody deeds and unscrupulous intrigue'.[4]

The next two centuries were to see a constant power struggle between the increasingly powerful lamas and the nobility and land-owning families. It was also a period which saw the founding of the Great Monasteries in central Tibet, especially in the environs of Lhasa, now the capital. This was made possible by the patronage and gifts of the Mongols. Huge monastic complexes, almost cities, were created, each containing many thousands of monks: Ganden, founded by Tsongkhapa himself in 1409, was followed by Drepung in 1416 and Sera in 1419. All Gelukpa establishments, they became monastic university townships and were known as the 'three pillars of the State'. Others soon followed: Tashilhunpo monastery, to be the home of the Panchen Lama, was founded by the first Dalai Lama in 1447 to the west of the dzong at Shigatse; the great monastic complex of Gyantse, Pelkhor Chode, is contemporary, again built near the dzong.

The increasing struggles between the sects and the land-owning nobility resulted in the ordinary peasants siding with the Gelukpas, preferring to be ruled and guided by monks rather than by a secular autocracy. Gelukpa supremacy was now unshakable and their missionary work in Mongolia reaffirmed Buddhism as the State religion when Altan Khan, the sixteenth-century ruler, embraced the Gelukpa cause. It was Altan who conferred on Sonam Gyatso, the head lama of the Gelukpas and the third incarnation of the sect, the title of Dalai Lama, literally 'Ocean of Wisdom'.

The expediency by which one of the sons of Altan Khan was recognised as the incarnate Dalai Lama Sonam Gyatso in 1589 gave more impetus to the developing theocracy of the Tibetan State. The successor to Sonam, Nagawang Lobsang Gyatso, to become known as the Great Fifth, proved such an astute religious, political and military ruler that he achieved autonomy from both the Mongols and the Chinese, which endured until the Chinese occupation in 1951. Religious unity was achieved by ensuring that the lesser lineages acknowledged the Dalai Lama as their titular head.

## The monasteries

The two great periods of monastic construction were in the twelfth century after Bhuddism had been reintroduced following the depredations of earlier centuries, and again between the fifthteenth and seventeenth centuries. The wealth generated by the Yellow and Red Hats led

[3] This theocracy was to remain until the Chinese invasion and annexation of the 1950s.

[4] Snellgrove and Richardson (1968: 149). Political machinations and intrigue have continued to the present day. Only a few years ago a plot was hatched to spirit out of Tibet the karmapa, leader of the Kagyupa school, from Tsurphu Monastery, where he lived under the supervision of the Chinese.

to the development of the vast monastic cities in Tibet, the hill-top monasteries in Little Tibet and the dzongs of Bhutan.

Whilst documentary evidence for the dates of the foundations of the monasteries exist, in many instances there is little in the way of documentation about the actual buildings. Study is difficult as very little has been published so far and although the Chinese in the 1950s surveyed the monasteries and made an inventory of their artefacts, the results are still locked in State archives. Tibetan choices for the location of their monasteries, most frequently perched on mountain tops or the sides of hidden valleys make access very difficult at best, and many monasteries remain inaccessible. The greatest problem, however, in the study of these magnificent buildings has been their almost total destruction during the cultural revolution in China and after the uprising in Lhasa when the Chinese destroyed any building of more than two storeys that might possibly have a military role. The country's architectural legacy was almost totally destroyed. Only a scattering of monasteries around Lhasa and the great Potala Palace of the Dalai Lama escaped demolition, reputably on the instruction of Chou En-Lai, together with a number in the countryside which were saved by their use as grain stores.[5]

Fortunately, Tibetan influence in Ladakh, Zanskar and the valleys of Lahaul and Spiti, now in India, although located in the west of the Tibetan plateau, has ensured that a number of the Buddhist monasteries from the late mediaeval period have remained more or less as they were built. Similarly the energies of Shabdrung Ngawang Namgyal and his lineage in Bhutan have left a number of fortress monasteries, the Bhutanese dzongs, the ultimate fusion of religious and military architecture in the Himalayas.

## Architectural techniques and form in the Tibetan cultural region

Tibetans build with considerable skill and ingenuity, using only the simplest of materials to produce monastic complexes that not only cover vast areas but soar skywards, storey upon storey. The basic building materials of sun-dried mudbrick, mud and chaff mortar, rough-hewn stone and timber, mostly fir and oak, are fashioned into buildings immediately recognisable as Tibetan, whether house, manor, palace, fort or monastery. Remarkable skill is needed to fuse these simple materials into buildings that can withstand extremes of weather, particularly wind, cold and snow.

Upon rocky or dug-out foundations coarsely dressed stone is set in a mud mortar. Between 0.5 and 1.5m in thickness, these stone walls rise to varying heights and adequately defend against rising damp. The use of sun-dried bricks, or in some cases of stamped mud, is reserved for the upper storeys. All walls have an inward batter. Wooden door and window frames are usually prefabricated in the forested regions of Tibet. Narrow in the lower floors, the windows increase in size with each storey. Floors are also constructed from timber and rest upon wooden columns or pillars. Decoration is often added in the form of wooden balconies and galleries reaching out from the upper stories.

The best clay available is used to plaster both the inside and outside of the walls; applied

---

[5] Dowman (1988: 8–14) states that of the 3000 or so monasteries that were in existence when the Dalai Lama went into voluntary exile in 1959 very few escaped destruction that in many instances was total.

by hand it is a very effective protection against erosion caused by wind and snow. Decoration varies from region to region and according to the function of the structure. Temples receive the greatest embellishments, whereas forts, commonly called dzongs, are utilitarian with the exception of those built in Bhutan. Labour was provided by the village and farming peasantry, with the more skilled roles being taken by the monks. Building techniques have remained unchanged for centuries, fortunately facilitating the expansive rebuilding of monasteries which is presently being undertaken throughout Tibet.

*Monastic types*

Hosla has classified Buddhist monasteries into four main types, although all monasteries are built around the main temple or utse lying at the very heart of the monastery.

The earliest form, built on flat ground on valley floors, consists of a four-way oriented temple with lodgings, storehouses and kitchens all enclosed within a perimeter wall, which may be round, elliptical or arranged in a zigzag fashion. Of these only **Samye** has survived. The wall here originally served both to isolate and to defend its occupants. Recently reconstructed, it appears at first sight to be crenellated; however, closer inspection reveals hundreds of chortens which adorn the encircling wall.

Hosla describes a second monastic form where the walled temple complex is separated from the other buildings necessary for monastic communal living. Cloisters, refectories, lodgings and storehouses are physically apart from the temples. Those that remain are found in Indian Tibet and include the monasteries of **Thiske** and **Alchi** in Ladakh. These two forms are from the early years of monasticism, before the growing role of the monastery necessitated architectural changes. Monasteries were becoming far more than religious retreats; functional needs brought about further evolution. As well as centres for the devoted, shaping and challenging Buddhist theology and philosophy, they became depositories for Buddhist texts, providing workshops for the monk artisan in wood-block printing. Buddhist fine art developed in the monastery along with astronomy and traditional Tibetan medicine; education of selected monks became a necessary prerequisite. Secular roles were increasingly performed by the monastery and its inhabitants: civil administration, involvement with trade, and the storage of foodstuffs, especially grain, given to the State by the feudal peasantry, became an integral part of the function of many monasteries. Involvement in these roles led to many monastic recruits joining for the security and comparative safety such positions offered.

As a result, by the fifteenth century, monasteries were composed of numerous buildings, physically separated, and without any formal arrangement. These complexes, straddling the side or top of a mountain, attained vast sizes, containing thousands of monks. Architectural form related more to function and the physical contours of the site than any other consideration. The theological role of the monastery is well demonstrated at the great **Pelkhor Chode** temple complex at Gyantse. It contained not only Gelukpa and Sakyapa schools but also those of many other sects. Here the straggling arrangement is enclosed within a huge perimeter wall, whereas in Ladakh and the valley of Spiti in Indian Tibet they are far more compact in order to provide a more effective defensive role.

Hosla regards the fortress monasteries of Bhutan as his final classification, with their orderly rooms arranged around a courtyard that contains the central temple or utse. Symmetrical of form with clear divisions as to purpose, these dzongs warrant separate consideration.

The ultimate development of Buddhist religious architecture was achieved when the Potala Palace of the Dalai Lama was built in Lhasa. It is one of the great buildings of the world and deserves to be considered in detail, combining as it does symbols of intense spirituality with the traditional trappings of Tibetan government. This centre of Tibet's theocracy shelters behind powerful fortifications.

## Monastic siting and defensive considerations

Despite the mystical, supernatural and legendary nature of Buddhism, the monastery builders seem to have adopted a pragmatic approach to the siting and building of monasteries. Their secular role in the early development of Tibetan expansion and unity saw them positioned strategically. Often built at the confluence of rivers, near to trade routes and at important crossroads, consideration was given to the needs and comparative comforts of the monks. Frequently built in the lee of a hill surrounding a fertile valley, the monastery, where possible, faced towards the east to catch the thin sunlight of these high places. Increasingly, over the centuries, monasteries gave up their valley locations in favour of mountain tops.

The secular role of many monasteries led to large numbers becoming very wealthy. For centuries the neighbouring farmers had given a significant proportion of their harvest to the monastery. Monks could also become engaged in trade, which together with the gifts and donations from pilgrims and patrons resulted in the accumulation of great wealth; this wealth was translated into monastic religious art, artefacts and treasures. The enormity of these riches is demonstrated by the incorporation of 300kg of gold onto the surface of the 26m high statue of Maitreya, the future Buddha, found in the Jamkhang Chenmo temple at Tashilhunpo monastery. The gold colour symbolised the loving kindness of the Buddha. So rich did Tibetan monasteries become that the Chinese labelled them 'the western store-houses'.

Protection was needed against bandits and brigands, from attacks by rival monasteries and lineages, and from the depredations of external aggressors. The documentary evidence relating to attacks on and damage to the monasteries extends over centuries. Samye, despite its protective wall, was attacked and damaged in the civil wars of the eleventh century, and there are records of the looting of monasteries by Mongolian raiding parties in the thirteenth century. The rivalry between the Sakyapa and Gelukpa led to serious fighting between the two sects; the king of Shigatse sided with the Red Hats to attack the Yellow Hat monasteries. A Tibetan army that attacked and besieged the Ladakhian monastery of Bagso was kept at bay for three years due to the huge grain stores kept there.[6]

Whilst the early monasteries were provided with a defensive perimeter wall, and at the time of Tibetan expansion and consolidation became associated with the nearby fortress of the ruling aristocracy, the ascent of the Buddhist lamas to the highest reaches of power resulted in

---

[6] The fortified, sixteenth-century monastery of Litang, in eastern Tibet, was besieged by the Chinese People's Liberation Army in February 1956. Defended by many of its monks and neighbouring farmers, it succumbed after being bombed and strafed by the Chinese airforce.

the fortification of many monasteries. Different regions had different needs and were subject to different architectural influences. They need to be looked at separately.

## The warring monks and the Dob Dobs

Whilst no comparison can be made with either the Murabitun or the Christian military orders of warrior monks, there is evidence to suggest that the supposedly peaceful Buddhist monasteries developed their own corps of fighting monks. By the fifteenth century, such was the complexity of the monastic city that monks became specialised, performing specific roles whether as farmers, traders, builders or carpenters. One group took on the role of monastic guards and policemen necessitated by the development of such large monastic populations together with their acquired wealth. The civil war of the early seventeenth century was fomented by lamas and the monks played their part in the numerous battles and sieges. The monks of Sera were regarded as being both clever and dangerous. They had raised a small army of warrior monks, known as Dob Dobs, who although feared were admired for their athleticism and martial skills. They undertook regular training and became a close-knit community. Inside the monastery they shaved their heads, but those acting as bodyguards to high-ranking lamas on their travels were recognised by long, curly coiled hair either side of a central shaven scalp. There is little information on how these warrior monks functioned, though they exerted political pressure that could be backed up by force.[7] There is much evidence of monasteries being attacked, besieged and defended by monks. Saskya monastery was attacked and pillaged in 1290, and both Drepung and Sera have been repeatedly attacked since the seventeenth century.

Enough monasteries remain to give an indication how monasteries became fortified and how Tibetan military architecture influenced the building of the Potala Palace and the Bhutanese dzongs; there appears to have been a parallel architectural development, a symbiosis in many instances. Dzong and monastery are frequently found in close proximity, best exemplified in the towns of Gyantse and Shigatse. Occasionally the dzong contains a monastery or theological college; Dechen dzong, guarding the northern approaches to Lhasa, contains the Sangnak Kar, a Gelukpa theological college visited by the great Tsongkhapa, and the fortress of Gyama Trikang contains a monastery. In other instances the monastery received a fortified perimeter wall with corner bastions and a protected gateway, the complex functioning both as a provincial dzong as well as a traditional monastery. The finest example so far recorded is at Sakya, east of Shigatse; here the Lhakhang Chenmo, or southern monastery, is surrounded by a square perimeter wall, 160m long on each side, reinforced by square corner and central interval towers on each side. That situated in the middle of the eastern wall contains the only entrance gateway. Believed to date from the thirteenth century it was the chief monastery of the Sakyapa sect and, surprisingly, escaped the attention of the Red Guards. The appearance today is probably much as when first built. In typical Tibetan fashion, repairs and maintenance remain faithful to the original.[8] There is also a northern monastery, now little more than a ruin with similar fortifications.

---

[7] Stein (1972: 141).

[8] Inside the monastery are wall paintings showing how the monastery was built together with any subsequent repairs and alterations.

### Samye and Chokhorgyal

Marking as it does the introduction of monasticism into Tibet in the eighth century, **Samye** has always been an important pilgrimage site, representing a continuum of Tibetan Buddhism for twelve hundred years. It has survived civil war (the eleventh century), fire (in the seventeenth and nineteenth centuries), earthquakes (in 1816) and the recent Chinese occupation, when it was turned into a farming commune and many of its religious buildings demolished. Much rebuilding has resulted and continues. The surrounding elliptical wall over 1km in length, with a height of 4m and a thickness of 1m, is crowned with over a thousand chortens or stupas. Four gateways are situated at the cardinal points, where there is provision for guard-rooms, or gonkhangs, for the protective deities. The central four-storey utse, containing rooms for the Dalai Lama and for the storage of relics, represents Mount Sumeru, the centre of the universe, and is surrounded by four 50m tall stupas and the temples of the sun and moon. The enclosure contains the lodgings of the monks, other temples, a meditation hall and a printing press, all of which have undergone or are undergoing restoration. The buildings are in fact arranged in the form of a cosmic mandala, the Buddhist version of the universe.

Whilst the fortified aspect is now much reduced, the mystical Yellow Hat gompa, or monastery, of **Chokhorgyal**, like Samye, built on flat ground, has the remains of its massive ramparts still reinforced with bastions and fortified gateways. It gives a good impression of how these flatland monasteries may have been fortified. The curious triangular enceinte, rather than the more common round, oval or quadrilateral wall, reflects the 'triadic geomantic symbolism of this power place'. Here three rivers join, three mountain peaks surround, providing abodes for the protective deities, and three valleys run into each other.[9] Founded by the second Dalai Lama Gendum Gyatso at the beginning of the sixteenth century, there is a fusion between functional military architecture and the magical symbolism of the location. The monastery is now much ruined but contains two temples and two theological colleges.

### Gyantse, the monastery of Pelkhor Chode

Once the third-largest town in Tibet after Lhasa and Shigatse, Gyantse is situated upon a crossroad; once a trading centre between Tibet, India and Nepal, its status is now much reduced. It is notable for being the scene of conflict between Britain and Tibet at the turn of the twentieth century when, in 1904, Colonel Francis Younghusband attacked and captured the dzong. Gyantse has retained much of its traditional Tibetan aura, ambience and architecture.[10] Whether secular or religious, its architecture is being maintained and restored in true Tibetan style, sympathetic to its past.

Surrounded on all sides by mountains and bisected by the Myangu River, the town is dominated by its dzong of the fourteenth and fifteenth centuries commanding the trade routes; Lhasa to the south-east, Shigatse to the north-west and Sikkim to the south-west.

Lying approximately 500m to the north-east, at the foot of the fortress is the great

---

[9] Dowman (1988: 257–8).

[10] The story of Younghusband's expedition during 'the Great Game' is well told in *Bayonets to Lhasa* by Peter Fleming.

Appearance prior to the destruction of the 1960s. Based upon a painting in the Tsuklakhang temple—

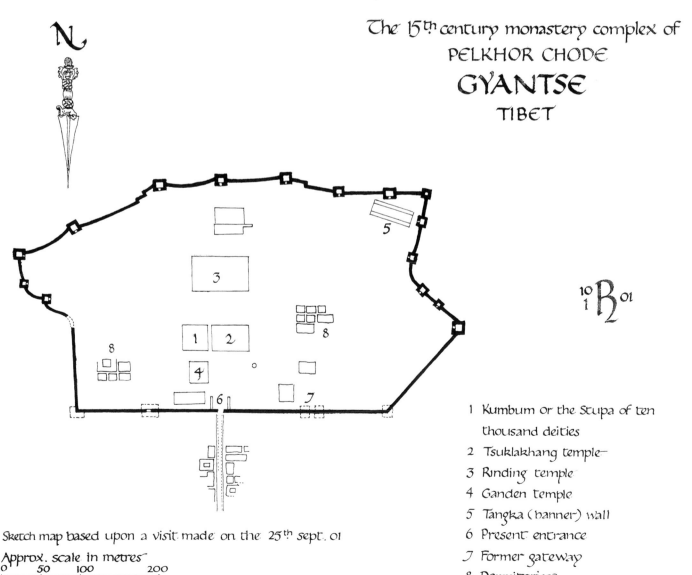

N

The 15th century monastery complex of
PELKHOR CHODE
GYANTSE
TIBET

Sketch map based upon a visit made on the 25th sept. 01

Approx. scale in metres
0   50   100        200

1 Kumbum or the Stupa of ten
  thousand deities
2 Tsuklakhang temple
3 Rinding temple
4 Ganden temple
5 Tangka (banner) wall
6 Present entrance
7 Former gateway
8 Dormitories

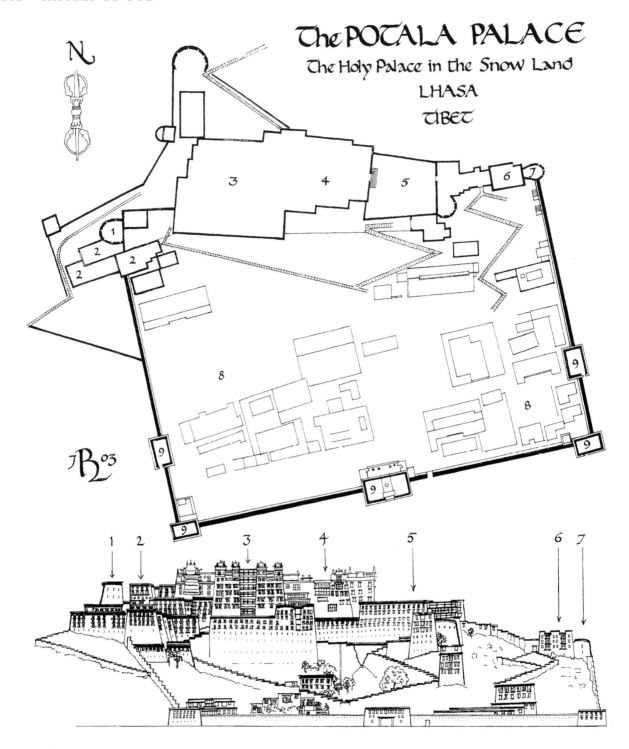

# The POTALA PALACE
## The Holy Palace in the Snow Land
## LHASA
## TIBET

1 Half moon tower

2 Dormitories for the monks

3 The Red Palace – the Podrang Marpo containing the stupas of the 5th 7th 8th 9th & 13th Dalai Lamas

4 The White Palace – the Podrang Karpo

5 The East courtyard, Deyang Shar

6 The old prison

7 Sun tower

8 Lower city

9 Towers

Scale in metres

0  10 20 30 40 50          100

The scale of the sketch map is approximate only

Other rooms contain shrines, chapels, meditation rooms and assembly halls, all sumptuously decorated and embellished with the finest work of Tibetan, Nepali and Chinese artists and sculptors and separated by numerous courtyards.

Ultimately the whole of Marpori, the Red Hill, became covered in additional buildings; rising to a height of over 115m, through thirteen storeys, it was until recent times one of the tallest buildings in the world. It still remains one of the most impressive. It measures 360m east to west and 335m north to south. With an interior area covering approximately 130,000 square metres the thousand rooms reputedly house two hundred thousand images.

The flat ground to the south was enclosed within walls approximately 20m high, containing corner bastions and fortified gateways. This bailey was populated by the laity, necessary to maintain the functions of government and the fabric of the palace. It contained printing presses, workshops, barracks, lodgings for visitors and housing for the civil service.

The substantial body of monks who surrounded the Dalai Lama were accommodated in the western wing of the White Palace, which together with the Red Palace was further protected by four huge drum towers, one of which protects a spur work to the north of the Red Palace.

Only wood, stone and earth was used in the construction of this most magnificent example of Tibetan architecture; the slopping walls are painted red and white and pierced by black-framed windows with decorated pelmets, increasing in size with each storey. The golden domes and cupolas of the chortens of the incarcerated Dalai Lamas provide a magical skyline. Its labyrinthine passageways, dark and musty, give access to rooms decorated and furnished in such a way as to show the continuum of Tibetan Buddhism and its art from the seventeenth century to the present. The nearest equivalent in Western Christendom is the Vatican in Rome and the Palace of the Popes in Avignon. The Potala Palace in Lhasa is the ultimate fusion of fortress and monastery and dominated every aspect of Tibetan life until the voluntary exile of the Dalai Lama in 1959.

Shelling by the People's Liberation Army during the 1959 uprising damaged the southern façade, the porch of the Red Palace and the Potala school; only the intervention of Chou En-Lai, who used his own troops to protect the palace, saved wholesale destruction during the Cultural Revolution.

The weather in Lhasa can be notoriously fickle, indeed Tibetans claim the weather of all four seasons can occur in a single day; the mood of the palace changes accordingly. Dark and brooding under the black clouds heralding thunderstorms, it has a fairytale appearance when covered in snow. It is seen at its best, however, when the brilliant Tibetan sunshine turns the palace into a dazzling mixture of white, red ochre and gold. The master of its environment, despite being surrounded by nondescript concrete and glass high-rise buildings of Chinese construction, it is a tangible expression of the devotion, beliefs and culture of the Tibetan people. In this respect, its future is as important as the past.

## The present situation

Much reference has been made to the damage and destruction inflicted upon Tibetan culture and its architecture during the latter half of the twentieth century by the Chinese. Despite a change of policy in the 1980s, allowing Tibetans to undertake rebuilding and restoration of their monasteries, the accumulated art and architecture of centuries has been irretrievably lost.

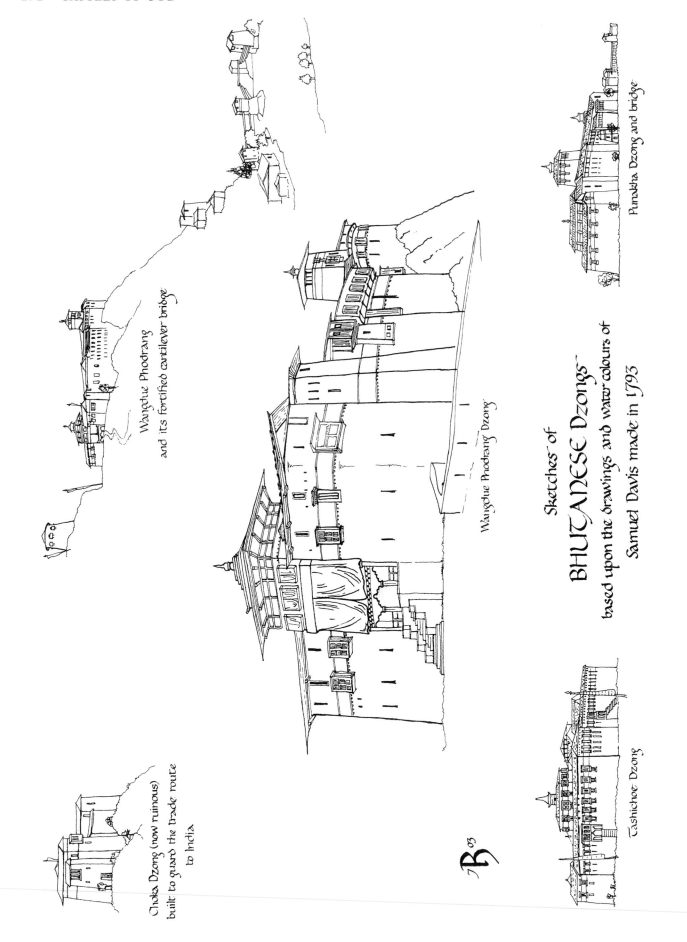

Wangdue Phodrang
and its fortified cantilever bridge

Punakha Dzong and bridge

Wangdue Phodrang Dzong

Sketches of
BHUTANESE Dzongs
based upon the drawings and water colours of
Samuel Davis made in 1793

Choka Dzong (now ruinous)
built to guard the trade route
to India

Tashichoe Dzong

further protect the heavy wooden and iron-studded doors. The rectangular main building measures 180m long by 70m wide and is unique in containing three courtyards with an utse of six storeys, each containing temples, known as ihakhangs, richly decorated by mystical wall paintings. Again the solitary entrance doorway is three metres above the ground, although the wooden stairway cannot be retracted.

Like all dzongs it is built of well-coursed, worked stone in an earthen mortar, and the walls are very thick. White's photograph shows that there were few external openings, closed on the inside by shutters, and none externally to the two lower storeys of the rooms arranged around the courtyards. The monks have taken advantage of the intervening century to widen these into spacious windows and balconies, especially to the upper rooms. The external walls have a slight inward batter and are covered in a white limestone plaster. Now galvanised tin sheeting is used to cover the wooden roof struts and replaces the original wooden shingles weighed down with stone river boulders. The eaves are so built that an airy space exists between the flat roof of the top storey and the pitched roof of the courtyard range; from a distance the roof seems to float above the dzong. This is a common feature of many small civil buildings and is used to dry grain and animal fodder for the harsh winters. The roofs of the various temples are surmounted by gilded pagoda like canopies.

The whitewashed, lime-coated stonework softens the look of this mighty fortress monastery, whose appearance is enhanced by the rusty-red woodwork of the window frames, balconies and roof supports, now embellished to varying degrees by symbolic wooden lattice work painted in vivid colours. Wherever a building in Bhutan is used for religious purposes a broad rusty-red painted band runs round just under the eaves and this is no exception.

Although the external appearance is impressive, nothing prepares for the colour and intricacy of the woodwork of the stairs, galleries and arcades of the buildings ranged around the stone-paved courtyards. Here is design, carpentry and artwork of the finest workmanship, fitting surrounds for the mausoleum of the Shabdrung built in the southernmost courtyard. Despite its richness and opulence defence is not neglected and galleries run all round. These are chemin de rondes and are loopholed at 1m intervals. Despite extensive damage over the centuries by fires and flood, each reconstruction seems to have eclipsed its antecedent in the care and skill given to decoration.

## Local variations and adaptations

Although there is a ready water supply at Panakha, in many dzongs water supplies would have posed a problem, especially at times of siege. It is reputed that the Shabdrung and later dzong builders got round this, not by building cisterns, but by building and excavating tunnels from the dzong to the nearest water source whether stream, river or spring. The best example accessible today is to be found at **Jakar** 'the castle of the white bird'. It now overlooks a small town near the foot of the Choskhor valley and is reached by a narrow path overlooked by the ta dzong. Acting as a barbican it is attached to the western end of the dzong by means of a round tower that, via a wooden ladder, gives access to a paved and stepped path. This path runs between high loopholed and stepped walls running down the north-west side of the ridge upon which the dzong is built for a 100m or so. Here it meets the top storey of another round tower where once again another wooden ladder leads to a tunnel running down to a well fed

similarities in plan, arrangement and function between the ribat at Sousse in Tunisia and the Teutonic conventual castle of Lidzbark in Poland. In a similar way the mighty Russian fortress monasteries are also a distinct architectural genus in having vast fortifications surrounding large religious and monastic ranges.

Many fortress cathedrals and churches combined fortification in such a way that externally the appearance was one of a fortress. Albi and Rudelle are examples from the thirteenth and fourteenth centuries in south-west France with the donjon church of Safita in the Holy Land very similar to the latter. These fortress churches continued to be built until the seventeenth century especially in the north of France where the church of St Juvin was built to serve as both church and fort. It was strong enough to resist a considerable force and protect its parishioners for a considerable time during the wars and political instability of the region in the seventeenth and eighteenth centuries.

Bonde credits the Languedoc with the invention of the fortress church and monastery in the twelfth century and points out that the adoption of the machicolated arch 'introduced an economical and effective system of fortification into Western Europe'.[2] This form of defensive military architecture was widely used in the Islamic east before its introduction into France. It seems likely that the close relationships and communications between the clerics of the south of France and those of the Crusaders in the East suggest that arch machicolations were introduced into Europe as a result of these.

Although a debate on whether the experiences of the Crusaders in the Holy Land and the development of the conventual castle had any influence on the development of Western European military architecture is not relevant here, the castles of Sancho Ramírez certainly influenced the military orders, however.[3] His early castle of Loarre, with its complement of monks, served as a prototype for the Holy Land, ultimately leading to the conventual castle of the Teutonic Knights in northern Europe. The refinements were restricted to military architecture with minimal alteration to the monastic layout unless the local geography of the site dictated otherwise.

## The effectiveness of ecclesiastical fortifications

Little has been written about the effectiveness or otherwise of ecclesiastical fortifications. What evidence there is suggests that they were at least as successful as contemporary, purely military fortifications of a similar size. The fact that they were built over a long period of time supports this view. Indeed in Russia and north-east Europe they replaced conventional castles and guarded much of the frontier in the Holy Land, Spain and Portugal during the Reconquest and the northern frontiers of the Spanish New World.

Views regarding how successful the rural fortress and fortified churches were in

[2] Bonde (1994: 174).

[3] Kennedy (1994: 188–9) points out, however, that box machicolations were incorporated in the Holy Land in both Islamic and Crusader fortifications from the early years of the thirteenth century but were rare in Europe. He concludes that it was not new styles of military architecture that the Crusaders introduced into Europe but rather new methods of siege warfare.

protecting their congregations vary and there is more contention. The majority of these defences were peasant defences built out of necessity by local communities. As with many static fortifications they were built in an effort to deter attack. There are, however, many recorded instances of fortified churches being attacked, desecrated, looted and burnt.[4] It is undoubtedly true that during this period many churches would have been targeted by the roving bands and nearby garrisons. The success of a fortified church in defending its parishioners, their goods and chattels would depend upon a number of differing factors. The number and desperation of the attackers would be deciding factors as would the scale of the church fortifications and the resilience and determination of its defenders. There is clear evidence that communities fortified their church to the best of their abilities and resources. That they must have been successful to a significant degree is demonstrated by the number that were built over the centuries. Where churches now have either no remain of fortification or only vestigial ones this is not so much because they were destroyed by enemies but rather that they were removed in the nineteenth century by restorers.

Where substantial fortifications remain, few show evidence of damage caused by a determined attack. Unlike castles there have been few attempts to slight. The churches in La Thiérache, for example, still retain their sixteenth and seventeenth-century defences much as when first built. In their case it would appear that many attackers were deterred or repelled. The evidence is that they were successful communal defences much in the same manner as the Saxon churches of Transylvania.

## Whither now?

Until a careful inventory is made of the churches and ecclesiastical establishments of Europe, much in the way that Brooke approached the churches of the Anglo-Scottish Borders, the scale, extent, distribution and types of fortification will not be known. This is an enormous undertaking, further held back by a lack of appreciation that this form of fortification exists so widely throughout Europe. Fieldwork in France has shown just what a wealth of fortified and fortress churches that country has, many not recognised as such. Why some communities fortified their churches and others did not is far from understood and church and parish archives need to be examined to determine the reason. Pagnotta, examining the fortified churches of Meuse in northern France, concludes that the reasons behind fortification, the number fortified and the patchy distribution can only be guessed at. The paper by Wright on the fortified church at Chitry in northern Burgundy is an illuminating insight into how this church became a village fortress by the addition of towers, a fortified cemetery wall and moats in the fourteenth century. He discusses the political ramifications and the determination of the community to defend themselves.

It is hoped in due course to publish a gazetteer, based on the research of others and on fieldwork; whilst such a venture is bound to be far from comprehensive at this stage, it will present representative types of religious fortifications built by the three religions under

---

[4] Curry and Hughes (1994: 113–14) record that damage to ecclesiastical buildings as a result of the Hundred Years War was great and widespread.